EX LIBRIS

Also by Charles Handy

The New Philanthropists (with Elizabeth Handy)
Myself and Other More Important Matters
Reinvented Lives (with Elizabeth Handy)
The Elephant and the Flea
Thoughts for the Day (previously published
as *Waiting for the Mountain to Move*)
The New Alchemists (with Elizabeth Handy)
The Hungry Spirit
Beyond Certainty
The Empty Raincoat
Inside Organizations
The Age of Unreason
Understanding Voluntary Organizations
Understanding Schools as Organizations
The Future of Work
Gods of Management
Understanding Organizations
The Second Curve

Charles Handy

21 LETTERS ON LIFE AND ITS CHALLENGES

HUTCHINSON
LONDON

1 3 5 7 9 10 8 6 4 2

Hutchinson
20 Vauxhall Bridge Road
London SW1V 2SA

Hutchinson is part of the Penguin Random House group of companies
whose addresses can be found at global.penguinrandomhouse.com.

Penguin
Random House
UK

First published by Hutchinson in 2019

www.penguin.co.uk

A CIP catalogue record for this book is available from the British Library

ISBN 9781786331953 (hardback)
ISBN 9781786331960 (trade paperback)

Typeset in 12.5/15.5 pt Adobe Garamond Pro
by Integra Software Services Pvt. Ltd, Pondicherry

Printed and bound in Great Britain by Clays Ltd, Elcograf S.p.A.

Penguin Random House is committed to a sustainable future for
our business, our readers and our planet. This book is made from
Forest Stewardship Council® certified paper.

This collection of letters is dedicated to my grandchildren
Leo, Sam, Nephew and Scarlett
for whom the letters were written in the first place

CONTENTS

INTRODUCTION

UNDERSTANDING LIFE BACKWARDS

Tell me, what is it you plan to do
with your one wild and precious life?

THE WORDS ARE those of Mary Oliver, the American poet. They have nagged away at me ever since I read them, even though it is too late for me to do much about them. It is not too late, however, for you, my young grandchildren, or for you, wherever you are, who are contemplating life's rich choices.

Arthur Schopenhauer, the German philosopher, once said that life has to be lived forwards but can best be understood backwards. Given that I am now eighty-six and ought, statistically, to be already dead, there may not be much of the forward part left for me but there is a lot of the back stuff to understand. I know now that life is too precious a thing to waste, that it has to be more than something to be got through, but it took me time to see my future life as an opportunity not a problem. I wish now too that I had been a bit more wild, that I had stretched myself more, taken more risks, been more imaginative. But I hadn't come across Mary Oliver then and her very pointed question.

I have written these letters in the hope that my thoughts on life and its challenges may help you to answer Mary Oliver's question better than I did. You are living in a very different world to the one I knew, but I suspect that the issues you come up against will not be that dissimilar. It is hard to learn from other people's experiences, but my reflections may make you at least pause and think before you act, or, sometimes, think again after you have acted. These letters, you might say, contain all the stuff that I wished I had known when I was your age, before I went out into the world and had to make my own future, my own contract with life.

I never knew either of my grandfathers. They died before I was born. Sometimes I wonder what they might have said if they had written twenty-one letters to me. My mother's father, my namesake, Charles, was an engineer with, I am told, a lively sense of humour. He was responsible for looking after all the lighthouses around Ireland. A lighthouse, he might have said, is there to light your way and to stop you hitting the rocks, just like these letters. Those lighthouses don't have people in them any more. Their keepers, and their children, have had to find something else to do. My grandfather, were he alive today, might then have smiled and said, 'That's life, you see, the same only different.' But what will stay the same and what will be different? That is the question my letters will explore.

THE LETTERS

LETTER 1

THINGS WILL BE DIFFERENT

I WAS RECENTLY given a tea towel to dry the dishes. It had printed on it a list of all the things that someone, like me, who was born before 1940 would not have known in their youth. This what it said:

> We were born before television, before penicillin, polio shots, frozen foods, Xerox, contact lenses, videos and the pill. We were before radar, credit cards, split atoms, laser beams and ball-point pens, before dishwashers, tumble driers, electric blankets, air conditioners, drip-dry clothes ... and before man walked on the moon.
>
> We got married first and then lived together (how quaint can you be?). We thought that 'fast food' was what you ate in Lent, a 'Big Mac' was an oversized raincoat and 'crumpet' was what we had for tea. We existed before house-husbands, computer dating and 'sheltered accommodation' was where you waited for a bus.
>
> We were before day care centres, group homes and disposable nappies. We had never heard of FM radio, tape decks, artificial hearts, word processors, or young men wearing earrings. For us 'time sharing'

meant togetherness, a 'chip' was a piece of wood or fried potato, 'hardware' meant nuts and bolts and 'software' wasn't a word.

Before 1940 'going all the way' meant staying on a bus to the terminus, cigarette smoking was fashionable, 'grass' was mown, 'coke' was kept in the coal hole, a 'joint' was a piece of meat and 'pot' was something you cooked in, a 'gay person' was the life and soul of the party while 'aids' just meant help for someone in trouble. When you think of the way the world has changed it is no wonder that there is a generation gap.

It is hard to imagine now but until I was ten my family lived in a house with no piped water and no electricity. We used oil lamps and candles to see our way around and had a noisy diesel engine to pump water from a well in the garden. There was no central heating, only a battery radio, and definitely no television. My father had a car for his work but we went around on bicycles or on our ponies. No, we weren't poor; my father was rector of a country parish in the Irish countryside. That was just the way it was then, in the 1930s, before the Second World War. I remember the day the electrician came to put a primitive wind turbine at the top of a tree in the garden. It charged up an array of huge batteries in a cupboard that then allowed us to have enough light to see our way around in the dark but still not enough to read by. It was a little bit of magic in our dark world. Five years later we were connected to the grid and everything changed. I remember my father's face as he brought out the electric toaster my parents had been given as a wedding present ten years before. He turned it on for the first time and, of course, overcooked the bread. Who could have imagined that the smell of burnt toast would bring such a smile to a man's face as it did to my father that morning?

Technology had transformed our lives. It always does and always will. The problem is that until it happens there is no way of knowing *how* it will change them. The internet was a great invention; nobody knew that it would lead to Facebook and Google. It often takes thirty years before the full implications of a new bit of technology reaches us. Today, as I write this, electric, driverless cars are one of the exciting new developments, but they are not just new sorts of cars, they will bring other changes in their wake. How, for instance, will we collect the money to pay for our roads when there is no more tax coming in from petrol and diesel? Will there be enough electricity to power all those electric vehicles? How will we stop our kids reprogramming the driverless car that we ordered to take them to school when all they may need is our password? Or, given that the cars will make it a priority to avoid colliding with humans, will those same kids delight in walking out in front of the cars with impunity, bringing our streets to a standstill? One thing is sure: the law of unintended consequences will have a field day.

AI, Artificial Intelligence, will be in full force by then. Will it destroy jobs or upgrade and support them? Probably both. With the help of AI, doctors will have much more information to help them in their diagnoses. The doctors won't be replaced, just virtually assisted. All those who now earn their living driving vehicles will either lose their jobs or find themselves upgraded to fleet navigators, supervising convoys of lorries or vans. They will be Individual Assistants to the Artificial Intelligence that manipulates those vehicles. My guess is that you can't have AI without a lot of IAs. Secretaries are already being upgraded to personal assistants until they in turn get replaced by their virtual equivalents, who will still need to be supervised in some way. Self-checkouts at the supermarket may be a primitive form of machine helper but there is always an assistant nearby to help those, like myself, who stumble in the process. There will be many more who only stand and wait, just to help us thread our way through the automated world ahead. What AI will certainly do is change the way we work and live, with more and more parts of our lives organised for us by algorithms of one sort or another, from our refrigerators ordering our food on their own to our wristwatches monitoring our health and renewing our prescriptions.

I worry about those algorithms. We don't know who wrote them or what their motives were. Some low-cost airlines punish families who don't pay to choose their seats by dispersing them around the cabin through an algorithm. US courts decide sentences with algorithms. Some lawyers claim to discern traces of racial bias but the consultants and firms that create the algorithms refuse to disclose the formulas they use, claiming it is their intellectual property. Algorithms may turn out to be the unnoticed controllers of our lives.

Whether you like it or not, technology will change our lives and you won't be able to hide from it even if you wanted to. The message from my own life, however, one in which I have seen huge technological changes, is that we will take the changes in our stride. What today seems fanciful will one day seem normal. You will cope, as I have done, as we all have, even the lighthouse keepers of my grandfather's time.

Forecasters predict that human skills will be confined to the Three Cs – the Creatives, the Carers and the Custodians. The Creatives will have the most fun and the most money, if they are successful; the Carers will be the most numerous because they include not only those who look after those in need, but also those who attend to our wants – in shops, schools, prisons, hospitals and any organisation you can think of. Then there are those who try to hold things together whom I call the Custodians. They include the executive part of the government, especially the civil service, but managers in every organisation will still be needed to plan and decide who or what does what and when. Even those driverless cars will still need to be instructed where to go. There will still be a lot of jobs, even more than before, maybe, but they will be different.

The truth, however, is that I cannot know in any detail what the world will be like by then. Nobody does. All I can tell you is that it will be different in many practical ways. Change is always there. Exciting, if you are up for it, but challenging. The Romans knew that. '*Tempora mutantur, nos et mutamur in illis,*' they said: The times change and we change with them.' Or, going further back, the Greek philosopher Heraclitus said that you can never step into the same river twice because it has moved on: '*panta rhei*', 'everything flows'. Or, if you want one more bit of old-fashioned wisdom, you can agree with Tancredi in Lampedusa's novel of Sicily in troubled times, *The Leopard*. Tancredi told his uncle, the Prince, that if he wanted things to remain the same then things would have to change. As someone once said, 'The status quo cannot be the way forward.'

What does Tancredi's remark mean in practice today? The first thing that has to stay the same if we are to find any meaning in our lives is work – and paid work at that. Even if some munificent billionaire philanthropist guaranteed us all a basic income for life we would still want to have some meaningful activity to get us out of bed in the morning. Doing nothing would be a waste of our precious life. Nor would you be content for long with a basic minimum income even though I will argue in another letter that 'enough' should be all you need. Money is one indication that your work has been useful to someone. There are other indications, of course – gratitude, for instance – but I shall long remember the first time I was paid for something I did and how good that felt.

But the way in which work is done is going to change hugely. That would be Tancredi's point. For work to continue it has to change its form. In my day most work was delivered by institutions, hospitals, schools, coal mines, steelworks, businesses of all sorts, small and big, the civil service, the armed services. Society was a complex web of institutions. Life for most people was a sequence of organisations, each of them a preparation for the next. They offered careers that, in total, were expected to last a lifetime and be followed by a few years on a pension, often provide by the employer. I joined one of those businesses, an international oil company, Shell. They expected me to work with them until I was sixty-two, and on my arrival drew up a chart of the sort of career I was likely to have, with a range of increasingly senior jobs in a variety of countries. It looked exciting. Many years later I realised that not only did some of those Shell companies on the plan no longer exist, neither did the countries, at least not under the name they bore at that time. So quickly does the world change.

No longer does any institution apart from the British civil service offer lifetime careers. Indeed, the average life of a business these days is only sixteen years. So how could they even think of offering you a job for life? Nor, any longer, even in the civil service, does any organisation employ all the people involved in their work. Long ago, in one of my books, I suggested that organisations would increasingly resemble a shamrock with its three leaves making up the whole. One leaf would be the core employees, the second the sub-contractors and the third the individual experts or occasional workers whom it would be costly and unnecessary to employ full-time. More and more work, I suggested, would go to the second and third leaves because they would be cheaper, would not have to be on the organisation's books or in their pension schemes. Increasingly that is what has happened. Some would say too much so.

What it means is that there is no longer such a thing as a secure job. There is no longer anyone looking after your future career as there was in Shell, planning your next move, the training you might need, even your medical requirements. You are on your own. Even if you are employed you will have to apply for any new positions that become available. Furthermore, once you are over fifty you will find those jobs increasingly hard to get. That is why I started to suggest that what I called a portfolio life would be the best alternative for people in that age bracket. By a portfolio life I meant a collection of small jobs, some paid, some unpaid but useful. Increasingly, however, a portfolio life began to be the life of choice for younger people, such as you. Sometimes it was because they did not fancy the controlled atmosphere of the large organisation and decided to try their luck outside. Mostly they valued the independence of the portfolio existence, risky though it was financially.

As one result, there are, as I write this, more people in work in Britain than there have ever been. At the same time politicians are puzzled by a decline in the amount of income tax collected. They should not be surprised; too many of those new workers earn too little to pay tax. Of one thing I am certain: life for you, all being well, will be so long that one day you too will have to go solo, or portfolio, if you are going to continue to work, as I hope you will.

Tancredi was right. More people than ever are working for money, as they always have, but in very different ways. No doubt those ways will change even more during your life, with automation doing a lot of the drudgery, but I feel sure that our human need to be productive will endure. Work will still be central to all our lives.

LETTER 2

THE HUMAN IMPERATIVE

DESPITE WHAT I said in my first letter there are some parts of life that don't change, and in many ways they are the more important things. Think about this: there are, as I write, three separate productions of Shakespeare's play *Macbeth* playing in London as well as one opera of the same name. Last year the *Oresteia* of Aeschylus was performed in London to a packed theatre and enthusiastic applause. Shakespeare was writing his dramas in the time of Queen Elizabeth I, Aeschylus, in Greece, almost 500 years before Jesus Christ was born. Novels by Tolstoy, Dickens, Jane Austen and Thomas Hardy are perennial favourites for television adaptations. Many would say that George Eliot's *Middlemarch*, written 150 years ago, is still the best English novel ever written. I could go on to list many more books and plays in many different languages that have stood the test of time and are still seen as relevant today.

Why is this? Yes, these works are well written and well performed on stage or screen, but there must be something more if what they were writing about all those centuries ago still interests us today. The answer, I'm sure, is that these works deal with the things that never change, with the way people relate to each other and the way they feel and think about life. Put two or more people together and stuff happens, not all of it good although much of it nice. People have been loving and unloving each other, fighting and quarrelling, celebrating and laughing together since the days of Adam and Eve. The human condition hasn't changed for thousands of years, despite all the technological and political upheavals those years have seen.

Those upheavals are themselves the work of humans. We have no one to blame or thank but ourselves, even if our best intentions sometimes go wrong. Most wars, even those of this century and the last, have been caused, as much as anything, by the ambitions and lust for power of particular individuals. There was no logical or compelling need for either Alexander the Great or Hitler to set out to occupy and rule over so many countries. They each had quite enough to occupy them at home. Nor, on another plane, is there any necessary economic reason for huge businesses to get ever bigger, sweeping up smaller enterprises as they grow. It is all due to the ambitions of the individuals in charge, however well intentioned they may think they are. Why, too, do the so-called captains of business continue to expect to be paid multi-millions of dollars that they will never be able to spend? What can be the point, other than to have a mark of their success, an expensive certificate of achievement?

On the more positive side, when Tim Berners-Lee created the World Wide Web, which he then generously gave to the world for free, he had no desire to change the world the way his invention did. He wanted to improve the communications between researchers in his field of work, to make things function better, not to make more money or to find fame. When Mark Zuckerberg and his college room-mates developed the first versions of Facebook he cannot have known that he would eventually be affecting the lives of so many or of accumulating so many billions of personal wealth.

Both these people and many entrepreneurs like them are driven by a creative urge to make something different or better. That they get rich or famous as a result was not, in most cases, the primary motive. They were just humans doing what some humans have always done: tinkering with things. Or with ideas: Einstein wasn't thinking of atomic bombs when he came up with his idea of relativity; he was trying to unravel a puzzle. Artists paint, compose or, like me, write, mostly because that is what they feel compelled to do. If they do it solely for a more utilitarian motive, like money, it often will not come out as well. Money and fame can often be the end result but not the original driving purpose. The different things that drive people have puzzled and intrigued me throughout my life. I know now that none of that is new; it is just the context that changes. What once drove the Medici banking family in Florence in the fifteenth century is no different from the ambitions of the Royal Bank of Scotland in this century: to become the biggest bank in the world, with, ultimately, the same result – they overreached themselves. People don't change, even while the world does. The really big questions of life remain the same, even in the midst of a technological revolution.

What is just? What is fair? Who gets what? Does he/she love me? Whom can I trust? Who are my real friends? Should I/we forgive or forget a wrong? Am I better/stronger/ more successful than him or her or them? Even in families these questions lurk beneath the surface, quietly ignored but festering away. If that is true in families who are locked into a common heritage, how much more probable are such questions in organisations of strangers? I have often thought that I would like to be a hermit, isolated from people and all the complications that they bring with them. But then I would miss all the consolations and affections that they also bring. Loneliness is the disease of old age and one that pills can't cure. Other people are a necessary part of life. You have to work out how to live with them, like them or not.

The first thing, therefore, to remember when any one of that list of questions crops up in your own life, is that neither you nor the question are unusual. Whatever it is, it has happened before, many times to many people. History and great literature are there to reassure you if you bother to look, read and study them. Great novels and the biographies of the great are the best guides to human situations. When I was writing my first book, on the ways and habits of organisations, I looked for examples of the ideas and concepts that I was exploring. I had shut myself away in a farmhouse in the South of France to do it and had packed the boot of the car with piles of American textbooks and research papers, for this was long before the days of the internet. Books and papers were all I had. I quickly found that most of the research relied on experiments with graduate students to illustrate their points, experiments that seemed to me to have little connection with real life. Luckily the farmhouse had a large library with a rich collection of Russian novels. Tolstoy, I discovered, had much more to say about the problems of life in organisations than any of the student experiments. The book, my first, went on to become a worldwide bestseller, partly because the stories from literature brought it to life.

I have spent most of my years without most of the technological aids that your generation take for granted. They make life easier, or can do, but an understanding of the human condition is the best preparation we could have for meeting the challenges that life throws in our path. The good news, too, is that humans have always been the same, with the same urges, desires, frustrations, quirks and charms. You don't have to reinvent them. As I discovered, you only have to read Tolstoy, and maybe Dostoevsky, to know most of it. I often think that if more politicians had read history they would not have tried to invade Iraq or Afghanistan or topple dictators in alien countries. History holds lessons that we ignore at our peril. At a personal level, my own rule is to think the best of people until you are proved wrong. It has led me down some false alleys but also produced some wonderful experiences. I like, therefore, the old rule of the Cold War negotiations: 'Trust but verify'.

You might like to try it.

LETTER 3

LIFE'S BIGGEST QUESTION

BY THE TIME you get round to reading this, if you ever do, you will be close to ending your long years of education and stepping out into the world. That is when, if you are like me, you start to ask yourself: What happens now? or, What am I now qualified to do? or, more fundamentally, What is life about? and Why am I here? If you are like me, or like most of us, you will keep coming back to these questions as you move through life, but you will have to start now at the beginning of the journey or you won't know where you are heading.

Of course, a decent education should have helped you to answer these questions before you left the cloistered world of school or university but, sadly, these topics are not part of any core curriculum, while a career adviser, if such a person came your way, is primarily concerned with fitting you into a slot where you might be useful enough to earn a living wage. That, however, is only ever part of the answer to those bigger questions. Why do I need to turn philosopher right now? you will ask. All I need is a job and some money. Yes, that is the How? But the Why? will keep nudging at the back of your mind until you tackle it. I had only two concerns when I left university – never to go to church again and never to be poor. I soon discovered that these negative ambitions were not enough to build a life on.

Why are we here? I began to ask myself. Are we just the result of an (often unplanned) conception, the chance union of a sperm and a waiting egg? If so, does this mean that we have no responsibility to anyone for anything? Are we any different from a cabbage in the vegetable patch or a lily in the garden, something that just happens to be there? Or are we, as humans, something different? We have consciousness. We, alone of all other species, are aware of ourselves; we can consciously choose our futures, think conceptually and work out reasons for things and events. Does this give us a special responsibility to do something with our lives, or is it just another burden?

Maybe you are religious and see the mysterious hand of God in our creation. If so you do have an obligation, I suggest, to live up to God's expectations, if you can work out what they are. The works of the different religions will give you guidance on this and even a list of commandments. For many of the faithful this is very helpful because this guidance sets down the rules and purposes of life, which – if you accept them – remove all doubt and anxiety. It's a big *if*, however, because you do have to accept the original starting point, that God is at the heart of things.

Some people duck that first step of belief but are content to accept the rules laid down by the religions as if they were true believers. That works well for them until they come up against the really difficult decisions. At that point their lack of belief in the underlying assumption that God is at the centre of everything will weaken their resolve to keep to God's rules. I suspect that this unstated half-belief is the way most people run their lives. There is a shared consensus between all the major religions on what are the basic rules of behaviour, starting with the so-called 'golden rule', to treat others as you would like them to treat you. Most people in the West go along with the basic rules of Christianity but would not call themselves Christian because they can't buy into the underlying premise. Britain, as a result, still feels like a Christian country although only 2 per cent of us go to church.

You could, alternatively, take the evolutionary route and say to yourself that you are part of a long trail of genes, that your only essential task is to pass on your genes to the next generation without adulterating the trail. To survive and procreate is enough. Evolution is not about progress or direction. It is only about adapting to the world around us in order to have a better chance of the gene trail surviving through your offspring and subsequent generations. That lets you off the hook of any need to have a deeper purpose. Your main duty is to live as long and as healthily as you can and take care to procreate – provided, that is, you think your genes are good enough to stand the test of time. If you do that then there is no other obligation. It is my sense that quite a lot of people think like that without knowing anything about the theory of evolution.

Such thinking, however, is dangerous. If everyone believed that our only duty was to maintain the process of evolution it would leave us with a society without any sense of direction or clear principles. This is why religions became necessary. They provided society with a form of social control by setting down a purpose for life and some guidance of how to live it. With the decline of religion in many societies we risk falling back into a directionless evolution. That would be dangerous and is why the question What is life about? is so important.

It's a small step from evolution to existentialism. Popularised by people like Jean-Paul Sartre, existentialism maintains that we are each responsible for our own values and for finding our own meaning in life, because we are human. 'Existence precedes essence' was the credo of these philosophers, meaning that we are all unique and different individuals who alone can decide why and how to live our lives. It is a tempting but, in the end, tough option. It is tempting because it sets you free from all the rules and dogmas of society. You are free to be yourself. That, however, is the tough bit because you have to work out who you are and what you think are the important values in life. 'Man needs meaning,' said Sartre, 'but he must create his own.' At first sight, this is a recipe for selfishness, unless you agree with Immanuel Kant, a German philosopher, that anything you decide for yourself ought also, logically, to apply to everyone else. He called it the categorical imperative.

My version of the categorical imperative is less rigid. I call it 'proper selfishness' or a modified version of existentialism. To look after your own needs and wants is right and proper, I argue, because you have to feel good about yourself before you can be of any use to others. If you only work to please yourself you won't be of any use to man or beast and won't feel proud of it in the end. On the other hand, if you haven't invested in yourself to begin with you will also be of no use to man or beast. Love your neighbour as yourself, in other words. Real satisfaction, I have found, comes from seeing the satisfaction in those whom you have affected. We seem to have been born with altruism in our genes; generosity is inbred in us. It would be inhuman to stifle it. It was Churchill who said that you earn your living by what you get, you justify it by what you give.

If existentialism sounds too difficult as a way to run your life, you could go with the sixth century BC Chinese philosopher Confucius, who did not believe in any gods and was writing and teaching 500 years before Christ. He said:

> You are humane if you can practise five things in the world – respectfulness, magnanimity, truthfulness, acuity [intelligence], and generosity. If you are respectful you won't be despised; if you are magnanimous you will win people; if you are truthful you will be trusted; if you have acuity you will be able to employ people.

These are good rules for living but they don't tell you what life is for.

Or you could look to Ralph Waldo Emerson, the philosopher of the natural life who defined the good life as follows:

> To laugh often and much; to win the respect of intelligent people and the affection of children; to earn the appreciation of honest critics and endure the betrayal of false friends; to appreciate beauty; to find the best in others; to leave the world a bit better, whether by a healthy child, a garden patch, or a redeemed social condition; to know that even one life has breathed easier because you have lived, this is to have succeeded.

I find much to agree with in this but to me it is the very least we can do with our one and precious life. We could and should do more.

In the end I turned to Aristotle, whose ideas have stood the test of 2,500 years. He was more ambitious in describing the meaning of the good life. He believed that our first priority is to be virtuous in our daily lives but then to seek for what he called *eudaimonia*. This is a tricky concept. Strictly, it means well-being or happiness. But Aristotle did not mean a sort of passive happiness or idle pleasure. Happiness and pleasure are very different things. You should not confuse them. Aristotle's idea of happiness was more active, more like self-fulfilment. Life, he felt, has to be about more than enjoying oneself. I sum up his philosophy as: 'Doing the best you can with what you are best at.' That's often quite hard to work out. What *are* you best at? And are you doing your best with it? Even then there is one more snag. Aristotle insisted that you must also be a good person; a 'virtuous' one, he called it. You may be a whizz on the computer but that does not mean that you can use your skill to hack into my bank accounts. Aristotle had a very precise idea of what virtue was which I will discuss in another letter. His point was that we are social animals and cannot live in isolation. Our deeds inevitably affect others. It's 'proper selfishness' again.

In my own life I have gone through all the stages. I started life in a rectory where I was told and believed that God had a purpose for me in life. If I trusted him and followed his rules I would find it. I gave up that idea in my late teens. Then, when I left university, I found that I had no idea what to do with my life. I had studied the classics and philosophy. That qualified me for nothing. All I wanted to do was to earn enough money to support myself and to enjoy life – the selfish existential option. I did enjoy myself for a few years and I did make money but the pursuit of selfish pleasure soon palls and I found that I was only a small cog in a big machine called an international business. Anyone could do my job. I wanted a way to express myself usefully but with more freedom.

It was time to go back to Aristotle. I now believe that we each have in us what I call a 'golden seed': a special talent, skill or aptitude. If you know what it is, or if someone close to you can spot it, if you then fertilise it and give it room to grow, it will eventually allow you to be the best at what you are best at, and if you do so while being a good and honest person, you will have a purposeful and fulfilling life. You will be an Aristotelian. In my case I had no idea what my golden seed might be, but as I said goodbye to my mother when I set off for South East Asia and my first job, she, who did not at all approve of my choice of career, said, 'Never mind, dear, it will all be great material for your books.' 'Books, Mother?' I replied. 'I'm going to be an oil executive; there will be no time for books.' 'Yes, dear,' she said, as mothers do when you know they mean 'No, dear'. Fifteen years later I had left Shell and my first book had been published. Sometimes mothers are the best at spotting golden seeds, although teachers are also good at it, or godparents if you are still in touch with them.

It is not for me to judge whether my books help others or not, but that is at least my purpose in writing them, while at the same time trying to abide by the rules of Ralph Waldo Emerson and Confucius, the best guides I know to a virtuous life. I was gratified, however, when I was once described as a good Aristotelian. Might I wish the same for you?

LETTER 4

GOD OR WHAT?

DO YOU BELIEVE in God, or a god, or in anything else? That is one of those personal questions that can only be answered by you. Let no one tell you what to believe about things that are beyond our understanding. They can only be matters of faith and faith is not subject to reason. Indeed, faith begins where reason runs out. It may help, however, if I describe my own journey through faith to the experience of living in comfortable doubt.

It was Julian Barnes who said, 'I don't believe in God, but I miss Him.'

I know what he meant. I grew up in a rectory. God was ever-present in our lives. He, always He, was the gentle kindly God of the New Testament, not the vengeful, fierce God of the Old. It was nice in a way to think that there was this person watching over me, even if he was often disapproving. When my reason told me that this was a fanciful concoction, I felt very much alone in the world, left to my own devices, forced to work out for myself what was right and what was wrong.

I also rather liked much of the trappings of religion: the rituals, the music, the architecture, the art. I decided that I could have the trappings without the faith. I started to call myself a cultural Christian. There are, I discovered, places that seem truly holy: chapels where good people have prayed for generations and seem to have left some traces of their goodness behind. I go to evensong on occasional Sunday evenings in cathedrals or chapels with good choirs and find it a great aid to meditative reflection.

So am I a fraud? I don't think so, because I believe that there is a difference between religion and holiness. You can have one without the other. Indeed, I have attended many religious occasions where any sense of holiness was distinctly lacking, while my most vivid experiences of something holy or numinous often had nothing to do with formal religion. These days many speak of being spiritual but not religious. I suspect that they are saying much the same as me. The fashion for mindfulness is another way of searching for some form of inner peace.

At one time, seeking to reconcile my agnostic feelings with Christianity, I argued that the theory of incarnation, of God becoming man, really meant that 'Godness', whatever that was, was inside us, waiting to be found and made to work. This is not unlike what Quakers believe. I was once asked by the BBC to undertake a journey back through my life in a series of radio broadcasts that was rather grandly called *In Search of God*. To begin with I described it as a fruitless search; there was no God. However, I ended my journey in a lovely monastery chapel in southern Tuscany where I found a sort of holy stillness, with no one there, just me – and something else that I felt but could not describe. I said that if Godness was anywhere it was there for me in that moment, because I felt most true to my better self. I got a prize from Lambeth Palace for one of the best religious programmes of the year – 'despite the dubious theology', the citation said!

I suspect that you will not be lumbered with my early Christian entanglements but I would not be surprised if you did not also wonder from time to time whether there was not something more than our dull earthly existence, some sense of the numinous or the spiritual that brought out the best in us. That, to me, is what prayer is: asking myself if I am yet in the fullness of my being. Wendell Berry, the wonderful farmer poet from Kentucky, puts it well at the end of one of his poems:

> And we pray, not
> for new earth or heaven, but to be
> quiet in heart, and in eye
> clear. What we need is here.

Religion, of course, has another role, that of maintaining social order through moral guidance and prescription. Moses wasn't the first to claim God's backing for his ten commandments. The question that a secular society has to face is what happens if there is no universally accepted moral authority figure such as God? There are laws, of course, but acting legally only takes you so far. Laws define what you can and can't do but don't tell you what you *should* do. That is the sphere of ethics. A good society would be one in which there was a common understanding of what was right and proper in human relationships. In the Western world there is a sufficient residue of Christian thinking to provide some consensus of what is right and wrong, but newer generations such as yours are beginning to set out their own guidelines, spread through social media, a development that can lead to relativism and a divergent society, with different groups asserting different values and priorities.

Christianity has also made a big contribution to our cultural heritage, whether we are believers or not. We (you) will make a huge mistake if we (you) ignore it. A friend who lived in

Florence told me how he once heard two young American women talking as they came out of the Uffizi Gallery, which is full of Renaissance art. 'Did you notice', one said, 'how in those mother and baby pictures the baby is always a boy!' I hope that I don't need to point out the gap in their understanding of Christian history. Without it they cannot have made any sense of anything they saw in Florence that day.

If such a fluid society of mixed values emerges it becomes critical that each individual forms his or her own set of moral standards rather than going with the values of whatever gang or group attracts their loyalty. Here, once again, I go back to Aristotle. Aristotle thought that there were two overriding sets of virtues, intellectual and moral. The intellectual virtues, he claimed, were acquired by inheritance and education, the moral ones through the imitation of practice and habit of those held in high regard, normally one's parents. The highest virtue, according to Aristotle, was intellectual contemplation. That, of course, was his speciality, so we can forgive him a little bias, but what I think he meant was that it was our first duty to work out for ourselves what a good human and a good life should be. In Aristotle's view, we should all be philosophers. I agree. I also feel that the study of philosophical questions cannot start too young and should be considered part of everyone's basic education. Young children are naturally curious and questioning, the necessary starting point for philosophical enquiry.

Aristotle went on to list twelve subsidiary virtues:

1) Courage – bravery and the willingness to stand up for what you think is right
2) Temperance – self-control and restraint

3) Liberality – kindness, charity and generosity
4) Magnificence – radiance, *joie de vivre*
5) Pride – satisfaction in achievement
6) Honour – respect, reverence, admiration
7) Good Temper – equanimity, level-headedness
8) Friendliness – conviviality and sociability
9) Truthfulness – straightforwardness, frankness and candour
10) Wit – sense of humour
11) Friendship – camaraderie and companionship
12) Justice – impartiality and fairness

Aristotle also believed in the golden mean, neither too much nor too little, and applied it to his list of virtues. Too much courage becomes arrogance, too little is timidity. Too much pride becomes boasting, too little is self-demeaning, and so on.

We can add to Aristotle's list the universal commandment to behave towards others as you would wish them to behave to you, or as Confucius put it, do *not* do to others what you would not want them to do to you. Add on Immanuel Kant's categorical imperative that what you think is right for you must then be considered right for everyone else, add in a bit of Utilitarianism, that the greatest good for the greatest number must be the right thing, stir it all up and you have a recipe for ethical behaviour.

Not that anyone will actually go through all that process before acting. You might, however, like to score yourself against Aristotle's list from time to time. Many of them now are combined in the new concept of emotional intelligence. This is promoted as an important set of social skills but I would also class it as a virtue, as the sort of behaviour one would expect from a civilized person. Aristotle insisted, like John Donne, that no one is an island 'entire of itself'. We are all members of the civil society, so should be civilised. It is more important to remember Aristotle's belief that we learn most of the virtues by imitating our elders and, hopefully, betters. Something to bear in mind when you yourself become one of those, as a parent.

Crucially, however, one should remember Aristotle's view that the highest virtue was intellectual contemplation turned into practice. Life should be something worked out and acted on. Hence his emphasis on *eudaimonia* or self-fulfilment with virtue, or, in my version, doing the best with what you are best at. Only you will know what that is, although, as I said in another letter, others can often know you better than you know yourself. It is, I believe, one of the responsibilities of parents, teachers and bosses to seek to identify your specialness, or what I called your golden seed, and then help you to let it grow. Education should be about bringing things out of you as well as putting stuff in.

I started this letter with God. I ended it with You. I think they are the same. God is shorthand for the Goodness in You, or, if you want to get theological, God was made man, the theory of the incarnation. Religion was a way to help you identify that goodness in you and put it to use. Religions turned into hierarchies and bureaucracies and lost their way. We therefore have to do it for ourselves. In that lifelong task I wish you well.

LETTER 5

EVERYONE CAN BE WRONG

I GREW UP in a world of certainty. Parents knew best, that was clear. Good children did what they were told. Parents knew the answers to everything. That was so even when the answer to my question was 'Because that's the way it is', meaning, I assumed, either that I was too young to understand or that they were too busy right then to explain it. It took me a long time to realise that this was often how one's elders said 'I don't know'.

It was the same when I started school. The teachers knew all the answers. Of course, it helped that they had a crib. Their textbooks had the answers in the back; ours didn't. The understanding seemed to be that our job as pupils was to try to learn and remember what they, the teachers, knew, or pretended to know, and then to repeat it back to them when the examinations came around. What that meant to my young mind was that all the problems in the world had already been answered and those answers were known to someone somewhere. These days, of course, you turn to Google to find the answers. In our home back then we had two shelves holding all the volumes of the *Encyclopaedia Britannica*, a fascinating storehouse of information that contained everything you needed to know about the world.

Or so I thought. Unfortunately, neither my teachers nor the encyclopaedia could tell me how to ride a bicycle, or what to do when I left school. Some problems, I soon discovered, don't have answers that can be found in a textbook. Most of the time, in fact, you have to work out the answers for yourself. Should I take this job, marry this girl, live in another country? Big questions, but no obvious answer or any textbook or expert to tell me what to do, which didn't stop other interfering people from trying. Later on, in work, I faced other questions, such as: Can I trust this person? Is this the right price? Is this idea morally justifiable? The questions got bigger as I grew older: what is a good life, what is the point of it all, do the ends ever justify the means? Philosophers have argued about these bigger problems forever without agreeing on an answer. That is because any answer ultimately depends on us, on our priorities, our circumstances, our willingness to take risks and to decide our own future.

My early education did not equip me to deal with these 'open' problems. If it addressed them at all it treated them as 'closed' problems, ones with what my teachers or some other authority figure saw as correct answers. The world seemed to me then to be full of commandments and rules of one sort or another, with awful consequences if you broke any of them. Some of them seemed frankly silly. The senior boys at my school were allowed to walk around the central green clockwise. The rest of us had to go counter-clockwise. Only the masters could walk across the green. There was no reason to it except to make us junior boys feel inferior and then allow us, when we became seniors, to flaunt our new status by walking around that wretched patch as often as we could. In later life I worked in an organisation where the central green was replaced by a series of restaurants or 'messes', some more senior than others – blatant evidence of inequality as I saw it.

These systems and others like them are all gone now. They were there to emphasise authority, the right of those at the top to tell the rest what was right or necessary and to correct them if they disobeyed. If this is life, I thought, I don't think that I am going to enjoy it. And it got worse. If school was frustrating, religion was worse. They, the religious authorities, really did think they had their answers to my bigger questions. They also wanted me to believe half a dozen unlikely things before lunch, or rather breakfast in my case. My father was an archdeacon and the rector of a small country parish in Ireland. We had family prayers every morning around the breakfast table, when my father read out a passage of scripture and led us in a couple of prayers. The Bible was the word of God and had to be believed. We went to the local church every Sunday where we turned to face the altar at one point in the service and recited the creed, which started with the words 'I believe'; I asked my mother what would happen if I didn't believe some of what I was supposed to say. The question was so unfamiliar to her, I think, that she did not know how to respond, but she suggested that belief would come in time if I just had faith.

Faith seemed to me, at the time, to be a big cop-out. If you don't understand it, or if you doubt it, just trust others to be right and go along with them. Meantime, if you just trusted the priests, all the answers to my big questions were there. There were, I knew, ten main commandments, or instructions, and many other pieces of advice and words of warning in the big book, the Bible. Religion, I came to see, was another sort of school, with its own teachers and prefects making sure that you did what they thought was right and proper. The answer to the good life was to do what you were told. In my teenage years I became intellectually frivolous and started to reinterpret some of the Bible stories. Mary and Joseph, I suggested, were just teenagers. She got pregnant by mistake; Joseph said it was nothing to do with him, must be a miracle. Like teenagers everywhere they arrived late at the census and had to make do in the barn. The baby turned into a radical teacher who threatened the religious authorities; they had him put down and, as a result, made a martyr of him that turned into a cult that later generations developed into a global religion.

I was secretly very pleased with myself but I never mentioned my revisionary theory to my father, or to anyone else. It was only much later that I discovered my ideas were not all that new, that others had suggested them before. No matter. It was my idea then; so what if it was not original? It was my first rebellion even if it was only in my mind. Perhaps, I said to myself, the priests and theologians are all wrong. Then I got nervous. How could I challenge the collective wisdom of two millennia of scholars and clerics? Surely all the wonderful buildings and amazing choral and artistic works were proof that the stories were true, that there was a God, someone worthy of celebration, or what they called worship. Or was that word itself, along with the buildings and the art, just a way of underlining the authority of the priesthood? Was religion, like education, a form of social control?

These were worrying thoughts for a boy and I kept them to myself, but they allowed me a sort of private freedom of the mind. I didn't have to accept everything I was told just because the people telling me had more authority than me. Oliver Cromwell, I read, had once addressed the stubborn elders of the Church of Scotland: 'I beseech you, in the bowels of Christ, think it possible you may be mistaken.' It was the sort of remark that I often wanted to make but didn't dare. Creative thinking by itself is not enough, I realised; you also need the courage to do something about it; like those two gentlemen of the Renaissance, Copernicus and Galileo. They lived in two different times, a century apart, but they both had the intellectual audacity to believe the evidence of their eyes over the authority of the Bible and the hierarchy of the Church. Moreover, not only did they think differently, they published their radical views and, in Galileo's case, stood up to be counted and suffered for it. Both of them flouted the Church authorities who effectively ruled Europe at the time, in the sixteenth and seventeenth centuries.

Both of them insisted that the earth went round the sun, the heliocentric theory as it was called, whereas the book of Ecclesiastes in the Bible clearly states that the sun rises and sets and returns to its position every day. Courageous and self-confident, Copernicus and Galileo trusted their own observations rather than the established theory handed down and subscribed to for centuries. They believed that those in power could be wrong and, crucially, they did something about it.

In 1543 Copernicus was shown the first proofs of his great work, *On the Revolutions of the Celestial Spheres*, on his deathbed, looked at them, lay back and died. One hundred years later Galileo was not so lucky: he was forced to recant officially and was imprisoned in his house until he died.

Legend has it that he carved four defiant words in the wall of his room: 'E pur si muove' ('But still it moves'). Unsurprisingly, these two men were my heroes; they encouraged me to think for myself even if it went against what most people thought. They also reminded me, however, that thinking for oneself does have consequences, as Galileo discovered. You may have to suffer for what you believe. Should you therefore keep your thoughts to yourself? It depends on the subject and the context. A proper caution is not cowardice but only common sense.

I made a point in my writing career to challenge conventional wisdom as I searched for clues to what the world of work might be like in twenty years' time. Inevitably I was first ignored, and then scorned and ridiculed, until, years later, they said, 'Well, that was obvious,' when some of my fears and ideas proved to be only too real. It was in those times that I remembered Galileo and Copernicus. Take nothing for granted, question everything, doubt the certainty of your superiors but sometimes keep your doubts to yourself until the time is right. I will say more about this in my next letter.

LETTER 6

CURIOSITY DOES NOT KILL THE CAT

IN MY FIRST job, working for an oil company in South East Asia, I was told to spend my first six months exploring the country and the workings of the company. I started questioning some of the distribution patterns and thought it my duty to suggest how they could be improved. But the operations manager was not my philosophy professor. He did not welcome me thinking for myself. The conversation went like this:

'How long have you been in this country, Handy?'

'Four months, sir.'

'How long has this company been here?'

'Er, forty years, I think.'

'Forty-eight, to be precise. And do you really think that in your four months you can come up with a better system than we can with all those years of experience?'

'No, sir, of course not.'

That was the end of that bit of creative thinking.

I took some private satisfaction a few years later when I saw that a new manager had created something similar to what I had recommended, but that was too late for me.

It happens all the time. Come up with what you think is a great idea and someone is bound to say, 'If it is that good or that obvious someone would have done it years ago.' It is never easy or popular to challenge orthodoxy. Heretics used to be burnt at the stake. Nowadays they just get ignored or, worse, dismissed. Entrepreneurs don't flourish inside organisations, even when their bosses claim to encourage creative thinking. The founders of innovative start-ups shrivel up inside when they sell their business to some big corporation and are obliged, by the terms of the contract, to serve out two or more years as an employee of the purchasing company.

Bureaucracy may be necessary for efficiency but it stifles imagination and creativity. Don't go there if you value your independence more than security, as I hope you will.

Creativity starts with curiosity. We are all born curious. You only have to watch a tiny child trying to make sense of his or her world to know this. But that inborn curiosity can easily be knocked out of you by over-protective parents worried about the health and safety of their little person. It can't be coincidental that most entrepreneurs are second- or third-born children, when the parents have learnt to be more relaxed. An enterprising person is like a good scientist, always asking questions: What is going on here? Are you sure? Can that be right? Is there another possibility? What is the evidence? Can we trust these data?

Entrepreneurs have a mix of curiosity and courage; curiosity because they are naturally inquisitive and courage because they put their ideas into practice and see failure as a step to learning; if something does not work it eliminates one possibility that never needs repeating. If you haven't failed you haven't gone far enough, is the message they take for themselves. I am told that James Dyson built 5,127 prototypes of a vacuum cleaner before he got it right. Each failure brought him nearer to his goal.

My own curiosity had been encouraged by my studies in philosophy at university. The course listed the numerous philosophers that we were supposed to study and I thought at first that our task was to learn and absorb their work as a sort of secular Bible. But I was delighted to discover that my tutor was not interested in me reciting their theories but only in helping me to develop my own, using the philosophers of the past as stimulants not authorities. It was the key to my intellectual freedom. Now I had official permission to think for myself, to question anything and everything and only agree if I thought it right. A good education would have given me that permission much earlier. Some, alas, never seem to have received it and go on reciting the rules of others as if they were sacrosanct. They are the unwitting prisoners of other people's worlds. Philosophy, I now think, is too important to be left to professional philosophers. We should all learn to think like philosophers, starting at primary school.

Science also starts with curiosity, but unlike religions, or my teachers, it never claims to know for certain. It progresses by assuming that those who went before, who created the current narratives of how the physical world works, were neither right nor wrong, they just were not right enough. The good scientist is always challenging current knowledge, pushing the boundaries, testing hypotheses in the search for a more complete understanding. In everyday life I find it useful to assume that everyone is worth listening to, even if most of what they say is, to your mind, balderdash or unacceptable. They may well be more wrong than right but there is often some right concealed amid the wrong. Even fools may know more that they think they do. David Hume, the

Scottish philosopher, suggested that truth came from argument among friends. That is also, in my experience, the best recipe for a good dinner party, although I like to keep the party to four or a maximum of six people, so that everyone has a chance to express their own version of the truth.

Another thing I learnt was that it was fine to be doubtful, to question convention or the accepted truth. I remember, in my teaching days, being a member of the committee that appointed new professors. One of the candidates was well known for his exciting lectures and for his external consulting work. He was clearly an expert in his field. Why then was there some uncertainty around the table about his promotion to professor? Then someone put his finger on it: 'The trouble with Richard', he said, 'is that he has no decent doubt.' You cannot be a good academic unless you are always willing to question the accepted wisdom, even to believe that you yourself might be wrong. To question your own beliefs and actions is often the best way of learning.

When, in my seventies, I wrote a memoir of my life, I discovered that the most interesting bits were my mistakes and what I learnt from them. I wish now that I had made more experiments with my life and more mistakes early on. My moderately interesting life might have been far more interesting and useful if I had. Looking back, my early education disabled me for real life. Curiosity was discouraged, even seen as disruptive in the disciplined classroom. Asking your friend for help was seen as cheating, and mistakes were, of course, a sign of failure. I grew out of it eventually, helped by the study of philosophy that also starts with questions and revels in uncertainty, but the tendency to accept the authority of others without question lingered for many years.

My wife went to a dozen different schools as she accompanied her army parents around the world. She ended up at a friendly but incompetent school with only two elderly teachers. She left at sixteen without any qualifications and knowing very little about any of the subjects in the curriculum. What she had instead was an unbounded curiosity that has served her well in life. She was prepared to challenge anything and anyone, to question whether something has to be the way it is, or whether it could be done differently. She thought like a good scientist and was often proved right. In many ways she was the ideal life-long learner. For her, every experience was a learning opportunity. But then she was lucky; she never had the answers drilled into her. Towards the end of her life she suddenly decided that she would never cook the same meal twice. 'Why on earth not?' I asked her. 'Because I want to keep trying something new,' she said. For her, life was an endless learning opportunity.

As my lecture agent she used to be enraged by conference organisers who often insisted on a time for Q and A (Questions and Answers) after my talk. It was always so boring, she felt, and ruined any mood of excitement that I might have created. Often half of the audience were behind the questioners and could not see who they were; the other half were in front with no eyes in the back of their heads with the result that the questioners were effectively invisible to the audience. Added to which the questions were only too often just an opportunity for the questioner to give his or her own mini lecture. 'Why not turn it into a running conversation?' she said. So she proposed what she called the 'empty chair' idea. She asked the organisers to put three chairs on the stage. I would sit in the middle chair and would ask anyone who wanted to talk with me to sit in the one on my left. That left the chair on the right empty, waiting for the next conversation-alist to come and sit in it. When they did I would round up my talk with the first person, who would then return to their seat leaving their empty chair ready for the next participant. And so it would go on, a series of short conversations in front of the audience. Everyone loved it; it was like a celebrity programme on the television. Just one example of how her curiosity led her to challenge convention and reinvent tradition.

Travel is one activity that helps you to think differently, as long as you are curious. One of our friends disagrees. She maintains that travel narrows the mind. I know what she means when I see some tourists who want to travel the world without leaving their own comfortable culture, staying in familiar hotel chains, eating the food they would eat back home, speaking only their own language, looking at the towns and cities they visit through their camera lenses without making any contact with the people living there. They return home with all their prejudices confirmed, relieved and pleased to be living where they do, minds narrowed not enlarged. Your travel, I know, will not be like that, as long as you go prepared to be curious, keen to explore other ways of life in other conditions. We, my wife and I, were sociological tour-ists. Ruins don't excite us unless they have major historical importance. It is the people that interest us, how they live, what they value, how their societies work. That is why we always travelled by bus or train and not in taxis, the better to watch people.

Sometimes the history and the sociology combine. One year we visited what is left of Persepolis, the capital of what was Persia 500 years before Christ. Its ruler, Cyrus the Great, ruled over the world's largest empire, twenty-seven different countries, and did so for thirty years. We stood there in awe at how he did it when information travelled only on horseback. It was an early and original example of a federal constitution, with some things controlled centrally such as the selection of regional governors or satraps, and others devolved. Cyrus was also a stern enforcer of human rights, spelling them out for all on the Cyrus Cylinder, which survives to this day. He sent the Jewish captives back home to Jerusalem, where he was acclaimed as a messiah, the only non-Jew ever to be so. As we stood there, I could only reflect that his management principles could well be a model for today's international businesses. That's what curious travel can do. It can stimulate you to think differently, to provide alternative models for life when you observe how other people live and work. I hope that you will travel with curiosity in your backpack as you walk through life.

LETTER 7

HOW CLEVER ARE YOU?

BY NOW YOU will probably have had enough of exams. Perhaps you have done well in them and can now consider yourself to be clever. Or perhaps you did not do as well as you or your parents might have liked. Do not despair. There are different ways of being clever, and some are more useful than others in life.

We have to recognise that not every young person, maybe including you, is academically inclined. Why should we expect everyone to be clever in that way and neglect all the other ways in which you can express your intelligence? Aristotle was the first to point out that there are different ways to be clever. He said that there were three types of intelligence: *episteme* (intellect), *techne* (craft) and *phronesis* (practical wisdom). Few can have all three in equal measure. Howard Gardner, a professor at Harvard, went further. He described a whole range of eight different intelligences, including musical intelligence, emotional intelligence and practical intelligence. You can, he suggested, be a wonderful musician but hopeless at maths, a brilliant cricketer and a dunce in the classroom. Howard Gardner would still call you clever, in your own way. Schools do you a disservice if they concentrate only on the cognitive intelligences. Don't let them. Real life needs more of the practical intelligences.

Perhaps if we called them intelligences it might help to give them more recognition and acceptance in our educational system.

High academic scores on their own do not always mean that you will do well in life. For a time I was the director of the graduate programme at a leading business school. Every applicant for the programme had to complete an aptitude test as part of their application. This test measured their numerical and comprehension skills. Business schools competed with each other to boast of the passing levels they required from their applicants. In my time there I found little correlation between the scores and the end-of-year results in our examinations and even less correlation with their success or lack of it in their subsequent employment. All the application tests told me was how difficult an individual with a low score would find the academic work of the school. On several occasions I overruled the selection committee's recommendation based on the test scores, because I liked the applicant's motivation and personality at interview. It was pleasing in later years to see how much those students achieved in their careers despite struggling with their academic studies. Their determination won through.

In whatever way you are clever you will still need to deal with the practical problems of life. It is the one great paradox of education that all the really important things you need to learn about life cannot be taught. You can only learn them by endless exploration. How do you learn to get on with strangers? How do you know whom to trust? How do you know how to plan your life? No teacher can teach these very practical things. You could, however, do worse than use Rudyard Kipling as your guide. I have found him very helpful as I encountered the tricky problems of life in the real world beyond the classroom. Rudyard Kipling, who wrote the *Just So Stories* and that great poem 'If—', also wrote a small poem for a young girl he knew:

> I keep six honest serving-men
> (They taught me all I knew);
> Their names are What and Why and When
> And How and Where and Who.

He was right. These 'serving-men' are there to answer the key questions that will face you as you move through life. The answers will be different on each occasion because each time will be different in some respect from what happened before. That is why education is both so difficult and so deceptive. A school or college will claim to be able to prepare you for life but it cannot give you the answers to any of these practical questions without knowing the particular circumstances.

Let us imagine that you meet someone and are beginning to think that they might be the life partner you would love to have. All of Kipling's questions now become appropriate. Is he/she really the right one? Why do you want a partner in the first place? And what does it involve? Is this the right time, anyway, to be pairing off? How should you put the question, and where do you plan to live? These are all open-ended questions, the ones to which there is no right answer. It is up to you. Sadly, most couples don't get around to asking them until they are already coupled up. My wife and I never discussed how our lives might evolve, whether we wanted children or which country we might live in. We were in love and just wanted to be together.

Or suppose you are thinking of buying a house. You see one you like. But perhaps you should stop and think: Why do you want to buy rather than rent? Is it the right time? Do you want to have to cut back on your spending in order to save for a deposit just when you are having such a good time? Where should it be? How are you going to afford it? Who will you need to help – an estate agent, architect, accountant, mortgage broker, surveyor? How best to choose the right one? All Mr Kipling's helpers are needed. At the very least they provide a useful checklist.

The problem is that you will have had no practice in using the list. You may want to go with your instinct and choose the house you first saw, ignoring the other questions. You might even be right, but Mr Kipling and I would advise you to think twice before deciding in order to let the other helpers have their say. In our marriage, my wife did instinct while I did analysis, running through Mr Kipling's other questions in my mind. It could make for big arguments between us, at the end of which she might reluctantly admit defeat, only to say, defiantly, 'But I'm right.' It often pays to put the decision off until the next day and then test it against all the questions to see if your instinct can stand the test.

The truth is that neither the school nor anyone else can tell you whether you should pick that person as partner for life or not, buy that house or wait for another. Nor can school tell you what job to take, or how to vote, even if they try to persuade you.

I have argued in an earlier letter that school and Google are happier dealing with those closed problems, the ones with known answers: How far away is the sun? What is the composition of water? What is the cause of malaria? A school can help you to work out how to get to Borneo but can't answer the question: Why do you need to go there? What the school should be doing is to help you to use Mr Kipling's helpers so that you can better deal with the practical questions, ones that will face you every day of your life, starting with: Why should I get out of bed today?

Schools deal best with the known world. But education can and should do more. Ernst Schumacher, who wrote *Small Is Beautiful*, the topic of another letter, put it well:

> Our ordinary mind always tries to persuade us that we are nothing but acorns and that our greatest happiness will be to become bigger, fatter, shinier acorns; but that is of interest only to pigs. Our faith gives us knowledge of something much better: that we can become oak trees.

Oak trees grow by spreading out into the unknown spaces. We need to do the same. A school or college can give us the roots but the growth depends on us. Real education gives us the practice we need to do that. The excitement of new technologies, including the likes of Google, is that they allow schools to move beyond what is known to explore our possibilities, leaving us to use Google to help us with what is known.

I don't believe in warehoused learning, the idea that teachers can give you all that you need for life so that you can store it away and pull it out when you need it. That doesn't work. Use it or lose it, they say, and they are right. Teaching does not always result in learning. I like to say that learning is experience understood in tranquillity, with help.

The experience has to come first, then the learning. Think how small children learn. We are no different. Schools do it the other way round. It does not work for most of the time.

In my imagination a school of the future would be a project-based, problem-solving arena. Students would work in groups on increasingly complex problems, using technology where necessary to provide information. The aim would be to provide opportunities to practise using Kipling's six helpers, as well as the experience of working with others, for Kipling's 'How' will often include co-operation with others. After completing the project they are then ready to reflect on what they did wrong and what they could have done better. Learning the right way round.

In time I would like to see schools more closely linked into the society around them. Some of the projects that they do could be done for real with clients in a range of local organisations, including businesses. In Britain there are now a growing number of University Technology Companies that take practically minded students from the ages of fourteen to eighteen and give them a mix of classroom and practical work with local sponsoring organisations. It used to be said that it takes a village to raise a child. Maybe the modern equivalent of the village is the surrounding network of potential apprenticeship organisations. In the past the young learnt about work at work, often missing out on more formal learning as they started full-time employment at fourteen or even younger. As it is, the urban village is too often a teenage gang where the skills that are learnt may be practical but very antisocial.

Educational reformers, in their enthusiasm for improving the cognitive skills of the young in the classroom, have neglected what you can best learn outside the school, in the workplace, leaving employers to complain that their new recruits arrive without the basic skills they need, including such things as turning up on time, assuming responsibility for their actions, using initiative and common sense, being respectful of others. Ireland is experimenting with a transition year at sixteen where pupils move outside the school on a variety of projects, practical work and travel with a basic minimum of class work. If your school does not provide opportunities to work outside the school I would strongly encourage you to find opportunities for yourself in the intervals between terms. The one week of so-called 'work experience' offered by some schools can be no more than a poor trailer for the real thing. George Orwell was once asked where he learnt all his wisdom: 'In the interval between terms at Eton,' he replied. It's true: so much of what we need to know in life has to be learnt but cannot be taught.

Until my imaginary schools of the future come into being, we must rely on the home to nurture Kipling's little helpers. The home is the real school for life. Or should be. There are too many homes that do not have the understanding or the patience to take on the responsibility for their children's learning and would much prefer to delegate it to the school. That, I am suggesting, is at present asking too much of the school. Sometimes, ironically, neglect can be the mother of self-sufficiency. Left to themselves young people quickly learn to develop some of Kipling's helping skills, but the 'What' and the 'Why' questions may lead them in the wrong directions without someone to steer them. I once said that the three most important roles in life require no qualifications and no formal training. They are the roles of politician, manager and parent. Of these the most important, in my view, is that of parent. We can get rid of bad politicians and bad managers but not bad parents, unless they are demonstrably and physically harming the child.

When you think about it, is it not odd that you will need no permission to start the process that will bring another person into the world, with all the burden that will place on the systems of the state until that person is at least eighteen years old, at a total cost to the state of something like £100,000? If you do start that process, whether consciously or not, then surely you have the responsibility to do what you can to introduce your child to Mr Kipling's six little helpers. No institution, no matter how well intentioned, can replace the day-to-day involvement and example of the parents, ideally both of them. Remember, too, that we learn most, at that age, by watching rather than by listening. What you do as a parent matters more than what you say. You are the role models for your child from day one. Think about that when you have your first child.

LETTER 8

LIFE IS A MARATHON NOT
A HORSE RACE

I REMEMBER IT only too well, the class list at the end of
each term at school. It ranked us on our academic performance.
I was a swot so I usually did quite well, in the top three and
often the first. But that only made it worse when I came in
lower down, at fourth or, once, much worse. It didn't matter
that there were a dozen or more names below mine, I had
failed. Not literally, of course, just in my eyes and in the eyes
of my suddenly worried parents. Was I OK? they asked. What
went wrong? Should they speak to my teacher?

It was no big deal, I said, I just did badly in some tests.
But I was worried; worried that I was falling behind, that my
teachers would be disappointed, that I had failed them as well
as myself. So I knuckled down and got back to my books.

Looking back after all these years I wonder why I was so
content to be measured by my progress in a race that was on
a track that my teachers chose, not me, and against those
particular opponents. Would I have done much worse in a
race against cleverer boys? As it was I was soon going to be
tested against all the other people of my age in a national
exam. How would I fare there? What would I feel if I failed
in that bigger race? How badly would I have done if the race
had been run on a different track, on a football pitch perhaps,

where I was an absolute dunce? Is life, I wondered then, going to be a series of competitions and, if it is, is it better to go for a tougher track or game where I would do worse but maybe learn more, or for an easier game where I would be more likely to win? What, in the end, was the point of all this competitive striving? Did it encourage me to learn more if I won, or to go easy as the winner? If I lost would I try to do better in future or give up, accepting that I was a failure?

That's the problem with competition, not just at school but in every aspect of life. In a horse race only the top few count, the rest are nowhere. As a sorting device it works well for the organisers but less well for the horses and their riders, most of whom end up as losers. So why do they still go on to join another race which experience tells them they cannot win? Perhaps they sensibly choose a lower-ranked race, one where they might perform better. Or maybe they enjoy punishing themselves in the belief that they can only improve if they keep testing themselves against their betters. Which kind of horse or rider are you? Whom do you compare yourself to, those who are better than you or those who are behind you? Are you in the right race?

Under the capitalist system the whole economy of a country is based on horse races: the competition for customers and resources. The losers go to the wall. The top few go on to share the spoils until they, in turn, get weeded out. Taken as a whole, society benefits, as long as the scoring measures the right things and the judgement is fair, which, alas, is not always so. It would be comforting to assume, for example, that those businesses which proved to have best served their customers with the best quality, service and price would win in the market. If, however, larger firms combine to lower their prices to force smaller businesses to lose money and collapse, the market is unfair. In recent times, online retailer Amazon has a declared ambition to be the largest shop in the world. To do this it relentlessly lowers its prices, partly because, with its volume of business, it can do everything cheaper but also, more crucially, to drive others out of the market. It is hard to compete against someone who is not interested in profit but only in turnover. That is why every market needs very strict rules to make sure that the competition is on a level playing field.

The competitive game can also be flagrantly misused.

I had a friend who, many years ago, started one of the first computer consulting companies, designing computer systems for businesses. It was the new fashionable growth industry and when he advertised for software engineers he got several hundred applications. He had devised a good array of aptitude tests to pick the best applicants but the tests cost money to administer so he needed to make a shortlist of the likely best. He used their A-level scores although he knew there was no evidence that scholastic ability was in any way related to coding skills or to system design.

'So why did you use A-levels then?' I asked.

'Because I had to find some way of reducing the longlist. I could have used their height or their birthdays but A levels were a more socially acceptable way of selection, even though it was irrelevant.'

You could say that he was using a flat race to find the runners in a steeplechase. I'm afraid that happens too often in life. First come, first served may work when doling out tickets but can't guarantee the best recruit.

It is because I distrust the distortions and misuse of what I term horse-race competitions that I turn instead to the marathon, another sort of race. For the lead runners it can be like a horse race, with winners and runners-up, but for most of the 30,000 or so who take part it is both a festival and a competition against themselves. They are not trying to beat anyone else, just to improve on their last time or to test their endurance. By competing against themselves they are hoping to get better, not to win anything. And it's a long haul, not a short sharp sprint.

To my mind, that is more like life. We set our own standards and constantly try to improve on them. More training helps, as does the support of friends and family along the way. It should be enjoyable too, and companionable since there will be many others alongside who are also trying to better their record. You can set your own pace; settle for enjoyment rather than speed; choose to run with colleagues or alone. Moreover, it will happen again, so if this year is a bit of a washout there is always next year. Life is long, like a marathon, and nobody is testing you other than yourself. Everyone wins, as long as they finish.

Looking at life like this might encourage you to opt out of horse races of all sorts. That is what I did in my late forties. I had tried three different organisations, ending up at the top of one, the smallest. But even there, I discovered, someone was still above me. There always is, I find: a board of directors, trustees, even the people working for you who are expecting you to keep them usefully busy, happy and developing. In other words, there is always someone else setting the targets with their expectations. I decided that my time with organisations was over. It was up to me and me alone to set my own targets, to start my own marathon. I became an independent writer and speaker. It was not easy. The first week I set up my small office with an in-tray and an out-tray. After five days I was puzzled to find that nothing had arrived in the in-tray. Then it dawned on me. Until then I had mainly been reacting to other people's needs or demands. Work came to me. From now on I would have to initiate my own demands.

It was difficult. It needed a new approach. Nothing was going to happen unless I made it happen. No one was going to write my books for me. No one was even going to ask me to write a book. That was the task I set myself and I turned out to be quite a tough taskmaster. I set myself deadlines and timetables for each day, locking myself away in the country with no holidays, no weekends, until I had completed at least the first draft. Because I was the taskmaster and I was setting the timetable it did not feel like pressure. I was running my own marathon. As the years went by there were many more marathons as I wrote more books. It never gets easy, but as soon as one finishes I can't wait to start another. Real marathon runners admit that it is compulsive, but because it is their choice to run it is always a joy.

Competitive races are fun when you are young. They are a way of testing yourself against others, particularly if you decide to compete in a variety of different races. If you lose too often, however, it can be depressing; while if winning is easy, the races become boring. I have met successful business people who feel trapped by their own success but have too much to lose if they want to stop competing. I should have stopped earlier, I now realise, and turned to competing against myself, not my peers, but in those days no one was running marathons. Now they are.

LETTER 9

WHO YOU ARE MATTERS MORE
THAN WHAT YOU DO

MANY YEARS AGO my wife and I went to live in Italy for part of the year. When we had been there a few months a friend asked us if we had met any of the Eustabies yet. 'No,' we said. 'Who are they?' Our friend explained that she had not meant the Eustaby family but all those people out there who, if you got round to asking them what they did, would reply by starting, 'Well, I used to be ...' and going on to tell you what they did before they retired to come and live in Italy. Sadly, we realised such people are still defining themselves by their previous roles in life.

It was our fault, of course, in the first place. We should not have tried to put them into that box, the box of their job or role. It is tempting, however, as we try to get an angle on someone who we are meeting for the first time. Like dogs sniffing each other when they first meet, we circle around each other looking for clues. It is wrong because we may then use the reply to land that person with all our stereotypes of the occupation they have mentioned. We might think that accountants are boring, that mathematicians are too clever by half, that politicians are devious or business people greedy. It would be grossly unfair to load our new acquaintance with all our biases before we had exchanged more than a few words. But we all do it, sadly.

I got my lesson when a friend recently asked me if I had met a new arrival in the village. 'You would like him,' he said. 'He has just retired and is looking for new interests and making new contacts.'

'What did he do?' I asked.

My friend looked at me, puzzled. 'I have no idea,' he said. 'Does it matter?'

'No, of course not,' I replied, a bit shamefaced, caught out doing what I accused others of doing, trying to define people by what they do or did. Call yourself an architect and you are branding yourself for life. If architecture is your passion you may be happy with that, but not everyone is going to be content to be branded in that way. Rather like a prison sentence, it can dog you for the rest of your life.

We are so much more than what we do for a living. One of the intriguing photographic studies that my wife did was to ask people to compose a picture of their life using five objects and one flower. It is a very thought-provoking exercise. You should try it. Most people include objects that symbolise their loved ones, partners or family. There are also reminders of their childhood, of their parents and of a hobby or passion, such as music or sailing or reading. What is missing, she sometimes found, is anything that signifies their job. When I pointed this out to one young woman who had an important management job in the oil industry, she replied, 'Oh, that's what I do, it's not who I am. One day, I would like what I do to be also part of what I am.' Point taken. I was impressed because she appeared to be an ambitious young woman. Sure enough, some years later she gave up her oil industry job to become a mountaineer, guide and expedition leader. I remembered then that nature and the outdoors had inspired the choice of two of her objects in the portrait.

On another occasion, my wife was doing this exercise with a young entrepreneur. The first object he chose was his wallet, stuffed with dollar bills; we were in America. He picked it up and plonked it down in the centre of the table. 'That's me,' he said. 'I'm a businessman first and foremost.' Then he paused, looked at his wallet lying on the table, and said, 'No, that's not right, the money is not important, it's my dream of how my product could change the lives of people around the world if I get it right.' I like to think that in that moment he had changed the priorities and culture of his young organisation. He had given his employees something that they could all believe in, because who is excited by the idea of making the owners richer? As an aside, I have often wondered why the captains of industry think that increasing shareholder value can possibly inspire anyone below director level? Working to make strangers rich is either quixotically philanthropic or just idiotic. Either way, it is unlikely to be a sound basis for any business.

All too often, however, what you do will dominate your life as you get more and more engrossed in your work, either because the demands of the job take up all your waking hours, or because you find it more fulfilling than anything in the rest of your life. I was like that once. The job I was doing was to create a new educational programme for mid-career executives at the new business school. The eighteen members of that first group were very important to me. The success of the programme and my future depended on their success. They needed all my attention, or so I thought. I left home before the children woke up. I came home after they had gone to bed. At the weekends I was exhausted but still needed to prepare for the week ahead. So I shut myself away to get some peace and quiet. When my wife complained, I would tell her that I was really doing it for her and the family; I said that they needed me to be successful in order for them to have what they needed. She was not convinced. I remember her saying that she would clearly have to become one of my students to see the best of me, or to see me at all, come to that. She had married me, she said, not the London Business School.

I came to my senses in the end, just in time. I have, however, seen too many marriages fail because one or other of the partners, or sometimes both, loses themselves in their work, putting what they do before who they are. Of course, in the world of 24/7 working and incessant travelling for some, it can be hard to find enough time to be out of the work zone and free to be your full self. We may like to think that we are the same person at work and at home but the reality may surprise us. One of our more successful friends took his daughter to the office on a Take Your Daughter to Work Day. Later I asked the young girl how it had gone. 'It was strange,' she said. 'It wasn't Daddy behind that big desk, but someone else I hadn't seen before.'

Inevitably different aspects of who we are show up in the different spheres of our lives. It is crucial, therefore, that we make sure we carve out enough space for each side of us to be seen. If we are honest with ourselves, it might just be that we are not needed as much or as often at work as we think. Sometimes, too, if we are honest, the workspace is more fun and more exciting than the domestic one, and we think we do it better. When you reach the family stage of life I would urge you to remember all this. One of the books that influenced me at that stage was called *Must Success Cost So Much?* by Paul Evans and Fernando Bartolomé. The book described the results of a series of interviews with senior business executives on how they saw their lives. The title of the book says it all: every one of them regretted that they had spent so little time with their family when their children were growing up and when they were needed most.

The weekend is disappearing. The universal break from work is breaking down because of that technology. It is not just hospitals, prisons and airlines that now work 24/7. We all can and many do.

Yet there was a reason for that weekend, or at least for the Sunday, or the Friday or the Saturday, depending on the religion of the country. Even God, they said, rested on the seventh day and reflected on his week's work, although he, unlike many of us, 'saw that it was good'. God was right. All work and no play, goes the old saying, makes Jack a dull boy and Jill a dull girl. It is not only play that we need. Most learning, as I have said, is experience understood in tranquillity. We need time and space to reflect on what went right and what could have been done differently in our lives in the past week or month. Without that reflection we will never change, or improve, or be all that we could be.

We need a regular routine for rest and reflection. The problem is that we now have to organise it for ourselves. You cannot expect the organisation or anyone else to do it for you. That should be easy, thanks to the new technology aids. In the past most people worked for 5 days a week for 47 weeks a year, allowing for holidays. That adds up to 235 days a year, leaving 121 days free for that rest, play and reflection. We can take one day a week for rest and play leaving 70 or so for the reflection and learning. Or we can adjust the mix and take more for family time and play. Nor does the rest day have to be Sunday. We often find it the quietest day on which to do our work with fewer interruptions, making Friday our day for culture and friends. The important point is that it is not only our choice but also our need. Without society's convention to guide us, we have to impose our own discipline on ourselves.

My own routine is to go on a forty-minute walk before breakfast, usually through the woods opposite my house. It helps to keep my body healthy but more importantly it keeps my mind ticking over. I think of it as 'going nowhere'. Most of my day is spent going somewhere or doing something. Here I am just walking, or wandering as a friend calls it, with no destination in mind. Nature at its best is very consoling, non-judgemental and tolerant of mistakes, as you can notice wherever you look. It is a wonderful companion. I let my mind wander as I walk, contemplating the day ahead and reviewing the days just gone. I then try, in that ambience, to rise above the daily trivia and look at my priorities for life in the weeks ahead. It is, I find, too easy to let other people's agendas define your days. I need to ensure that my instinct to be busy and to say 'yes' to all requests does not take over my life.

It is, you might say, a form of walking mindfulness, only I see it not as withdrawing from the world but taking back control by re-establishing my priorities. To do that I have to escape my regular workspace and go into another space which works to a different rhythm and where the sounds of keyboard clicks are replaced by birdsong and the rustle of leaves in the wind. A friend of mine, David Pearl, has created a novel social enterprise called Street Wisdom. He, or increasingly anyone, invites anyone who logs on to the website of that name to join a group that will meet at a specified time and place in a town or city. They will be invited to walk the nearby streets for a couple of hours, quietly observing what goes on, speaking to those they meet if they want to, reflecting on all the richness and variety of life that they encounter. They then return to discuss in the group the impact that the experience has had on them. It is all free and is now happening in towns and cities around the world. People, it seems, welcome the simple structure that it provides for a walk to nowhere.

LETTER 10

KEEP IT SMALL

IN 1973 ERNST SCHUMACHER, a British/Swiss economist, wrote a book called *Small Is Beautiful*. The title was the inspired suggestion of an editor, although the main thrust of the book was contained in its subtitle: 'Economics as if People Mattered'. I was tempted to steal that subtitle for my own book three years later on organisations and call it 'Management as if People Mattered', because that was at the heart of what my message was going to be. I came to realise that if people truly mattered then it was better that they worked, if at all possible, in situations where everyone could know each other. For how can you trust or rely on someone whom you never meet? Humans need human-sized groups to be at their best. Small is better if not essential to get the job done properly.

I was largely influenced by my own experience. I spent the first seven years of my working life in a subsidiary of the big Shell Company, first in Singapore and then Malaysia. In those days it was, by Shell standards, a small company. Indeed, company was the right word, because it felt like a group of companions. It was a work family. We were well looked after; we all knew each other, almost too well sometimes, like a real family. I then returned to London, to a job in the headquarters of the Shell Group. I shared an office with Gerry, with a nice view of the Thames below. Gerry was the only person that I got to know at all well. Everyone else was an official of the business. When you think of someone as an official it means that you only come across them in their official role. You don't know, and usually don't care, what makes them tick as a human being. All that personal stuff is hidden behind their official title and duties. Public officials such as police officers will often wear uniforms to make it clear that they are there in their official capacity not as private individuals.

We didn't wear uniforms in Shell, although there was an unspoken dress code of grey suits and ties, suitably anonymous. We also concealed our private selves behind our job titles. The door of our office had a big brass plate on the outside with the official name of our little department: 'MKR/35'. Under it there were two slots for two bits of card with our names printed on them. The message was clear to me. What mattered was the department; the names were replaceable. When we wrote memos or letters to other departments they had to be from MKR/35, not from Gerry or Charles. Gerry did not seem to mind this. I did. I was not me, but a 'temporary role occupant', an impersonal word typical of a bureaucracy where the job mattered more than the individual. I was no longer in a family of companions but in a complicated network of boxes called an organisation, a machine for organising work. I did not enjoy being part of a machine.

I did understand that the task of organising the production and delivery of a wide range of oil products around the world was complicated; it needed to be done in a systematic way, with rules and procedures, but I did not have to like it. I was given a so-called 'role description' for my job as one small part of that system. It was three pages long, describing in detail what I was to do. At the end was a line 'Authority:

Authority to incur expenditure on own account up to a maximum of ten pounds.' That was to be the limit of my creativity or initiative. To me it showed how much they trusted me. Not much, I could see. I wrote a book some years later that I called *The Empty Raincoat* after a sculpture that I had seen in a sculpture garden in Minneapolis. It symbolised, I felt, the way large organisations saw their people. They were humans on the outside but nobody inside, pawns on the corporate chessboard, to be moved around as the game progressed.

The good news today is that many of those jobs no longer exist. The new technology does it all. In theory humans aren't needed. Nobody should regret that. You would never have enjoyed the job that I had any more than I did. Nevertheless, large organisations will still continue to exist in some form and that poses a challenge. Humans should only be used to do what humans do best: combining together to get things done as sensibly and creatively and effectively as possible. The technology should not try to do what humans do better, and vice versa. We combine best in families, even when we disagree, and in villages of families. Great cities are collections of villages that in turn are collections of families. Edmund Burke, the great Whig politician/philosopher, talked of the 'small platoons' that make up society. He was right.

Why are villages and platoons better than mass organisations? Because they are human scale: they allow you to be a person, not a cog. Professor Robin Dunbar has studied a wide range of human groups down the ages, from early society to the modern day. He has come up with the Dunbar number: 150. This, he says, is the largest 'number of people we [can] know personally, whom we can trust, whom we feel some emotional affinity for ... It has been 150 for as long as we have been a species.' As I said in another letter, humans don't change.

In my experience 150 is pushing it. I like the other bit of Dunbar's research, where he says that our levels of intimacy go up in multiples of three. We may have just five people whom we know intimately and trust implicitly: our best friends. At the next levels there are 15 good friends or mates whom we are always delighted to be with, 45 whom we see occasionally, perhaps work with, and 135 that make up our Christmas card or Facebook list of friends whom we want to keep in touch with. I have found that, for me, forty-five works best as the maximum size of a work group. And when a manager tells me that the organisation has grown to one hundred people, I say, 'Be careful, you will now start to introduce specialisations and departments, you will become more bureaucratic, a machine.'

We need large organisations. Now more than ever as the world increasingly becomes one big marketplace. Oil companies such as Shell, car manufacturers, pharmaceutical businesses, steelworks and many others like them have to employ a lot of people to get the work done. The new giants such as Facebook only work if everyone signs up to them, so they swallow up competitors as soon as they appear. The winner takes all. China and Iran may try to protect their economies from foreign global giants but technology breaks through in the end. Big, I'm afraid, is here to stay.

Can these city-like organisations restructure themselves into collections of villages that are linked together by the new information technology? My guess is that the organisations will have to start doing just that if they want to attract the best and brightest of the new generation. Already young people are turning away from the traditional pyramid organisations in which you clamber your way up the hierarchy over the years. The world of work is increasingly going to realise that small is better.

Such organisations already exist. Small start-ups keep things small, until they become successful. But large organisations are also trying. Haier, in China, employs over 70,000 people. It is large. It makes things, physical things like refrigerators, ovens, domestic equipment, things that might seem ripe for industrial-style mass organisation. But Haier is largely made up of 2,000 autonomous groups. These groups of seven to ten people organise their own work and if they can make improvements or boost their sales, they can keep some of the savings or profit. I am a great believer in the federal principle as the best way for all organisations, business as well as political, to grow big while keeping its bits small. The British are fierce opponents of federalism, which is strange since it is the form adopted by all their departing colonies, from America through to Australia, and its defeated enemies such as Germany where federalism works all too well.

Federalism, despite British fears, does not mean centralisation but the reverse. Its dominating principle is subsidiarity, an ugly term which effectively means reverse delegation in that power is considered to lie in the small parts of the organisation, who then delegate to the centre only the things that the centre can do better for them all. It is the only way that a city of small villages can work. *The Federalist Papers*, a collection of essays put together by the founding fathers who drew up the American constitution, is well worth reading if you ever get interested in politics. After all, you would have to admit that America has done quite well by following those ideas.

My family lives in a large Victorian house on the edge of London. When it was first built, in 1890, it was built for a family who all lived there with their servants. Between them they occupied the whole house, with the servants at the top and in the basement or the coach house next door. It was what is called a total organisation; everyone concerned with the family lived together, with a hierarchy of responsibility, starting with the head of the household. Today the property is divided into eight apartments whose occupants all live separate independent lives. I have calculated that the same number of people live there now as in 1890. That house, I suggest, is just like the organisations of the future; it still looks the same on the outside, one big house, but inside it is made up of independent groups who use some common facilities but are essentially independent, small but linked together.

Young people today often start off their working lives in an organisation, be it in business, government or the charity sector. That is sensible, for a time. I see such organisations as the graduate schools for work. They introduce young people to the necessary disciplines of work, the routines and systems, the need to sell as well as produce, the numbers that matter and the people who can be relied upon. If you go this way you will, I predict, soon yearn for the intimacy of the small group and the space to use your initiative to make a difference. If the organisation does not provide this you should move on, having finished your graduate apprenticeship. Humans are not meant to be machines.

LETTER 11

YOU ARE NOT A HUMAN RESOURCE

ORGANISATIONS CAN BE tough places. I have even suggested that they are on occasion prisons for the human soul. A bit harsh, perhaps? But I wonder. I do remember that when I was offered a job by Shell after leaving university, I sent a telegram to my parents in Ireland saying 'Life is Solved.' I really thought it was, because Shell had assumed that I would spend all my working life with them; they would see to it that I got paid, did useful work and would continue to be paid after I retired. There was nothing left to worry about.

That was until I married. When they wanted to post me to Liberia in West Africa, I saw it as one more step in the ladder of promotion. My wife saw it differently. She said, 'I did not realise that I was marrying a man who would go wherever he was told to go, would do whatever they wanted, whoever "they" were, and would judge his whole life by his rank in their organisation. Did you know you were that sort of man?' That was the first time I realised I had made what I was later to call a pact with the devil. In exchange for the promise of financial security and guaranteed work, I had sold my time to complete strangers with my permission for them to use that time for their own purposes; those purposes being partly, or even mainly in some cases, to enrich their investors. I had thought they were giving ME something, ignoring that I had in effect given away my birthright, or my right to do what I wanted with my own life.

Of course, most organisations do not see it that way. They see it as a consensual arrangement from which both sides gain. Some lean over backwards to make their place of work more user-friendly, with fringe benefits ranging from free food, health- and childcare to meditation classes, sports facilities, community volunteer opportunities – all a well-intentioned attempt to provide a whole-of-life environment. Yet a comfortable, even luxurious prison is still a prison; you will still have given the organisation the right to use your time as they see fit. The effective use of that time is what is then called 'management'. The problem is that managing your time inevitably involves managing you and my guess is that neither you nor anyone else likes to be managed and controlled by others, particularly if you don't know some of them.

Think about this: any organisation whose key assets are talented or skilled people – universities, theatres, law firms, churches – don't use the word 'manager' to describe the people in charge. They call them deans, senior partners, bishops, directors or team leaders. The title of manager is only used of those who are in charge of things, not people, that is the physical or inanimate parts of the organisation: the transport, the information systems, the building. Instinctively these organisations recognise that people don't like to be 'managed' and avoid the word wherever possible. The word implies that you are a resource, something that is controlled by others, a 'thing' to be used and deployed as others see fit. The unfortunate term 'human resources' only encourages this way of thinking. As individuals we like to think that we have choices, that we are not slaves who have sold their time to others. In signing away our right to our time we have ceded power over the most active part of our lives to others in the conviction that it is in our interest to do so. That is why I call it the devil's contract.

It gets worse. Treat people like things and they behave like things. They do only what they have to do to keep their side of the contract. As part of a holiday job my son took on a part-time job moving furniture at the local hospital. Applying his teenage brain to the task he and his co-workers had been given, he pointed to some logical changes that would allow the job to be done in half the time. His fellow workers were outraged. Why do the work quicker, they said, when they were paid by the hour? Why should they work more than they had to for the benefit of others? A trivial example but one that is all too common in organisations of all types and sizes. Observing this tendency to adapt the work to suit the convenience of the workers, the management builds in incentives to promote faster working, only to find then that quality suffers. They therefore balance the incentives for faster work with quality controls that highlight inferior work. So it goes on, a mixture of carrots and sticks as if they were training dogs or manipulating rats in a cage. Of course, say the management theorists, good managers recognise this, they lead by persuasion and encouragement. Excellent, but why not then call it leadership or some other word – but not management, lest you risk being seen as a self-interested manipulator.

Because organisations do need to be organised. The flow of work needs to be compartmentalised and people need to know what they are required to do, by when and to what standard; but that is managing the work, not the individuals.

The difference is crucial. If I know what I am meant to be doing and I believe it to be either useful or necessary, I will do it without someone looking over my shoulder. I remember Mel, a colleague of mine at the London Business School. He specialised in the management of groups and teams. Then one day he left to start his own restaurant. A year later I bumped into him. 'It must be nice,' I said, 'to be able to practise all that you were preaching back at the School.' 'It's funny,' he replied, 'but I found that if you choose the right people to start with, and if they know what they are meant to do, they just get on with it without any checking or fuss.' I call that leadership: creating the conditions for good work, choosing the right people and setting them standards of achievement that they can understand, and rewarding them when they meet them. You may say that I am just playing with words but words describe the world, even the local world of the organisation. I now believe that WORK needs to be ORGANISED, that THINGS should be MANAGED, but that PEOPLE can only be encouraged, inspired and LED. By 'things', I mean the buildings, information systems or anything physical.

There are those, however, who prefer to elevate the idea of management to include the organising and the leading. Management, said the great Peter Drucker, is a human and social art. Much though I admire the thinking and writings of Drucker, I do wish that he had avoided that word because it has been so misinterpreted and abused by people who see it as an excuse to exercise their power over their fellow humans. Words do matter. They change behaviour. They shape our thinking because of the implicit messages they send; then our thoughts shape our actions. Call someone a human resource and it is only one step further to assume that he or she can be treated like other things, be oiled and fuelled, perhaps, but also controlled and even dispensed with when surplus to requirements. Good managers know this, you may say, but language can trick you into behaving in ways you would normally avoid. Words are devious, dangerous things. Always watch your language lest you send messages that you never intended.

One day you in your turn may find yourself responsible for organising the work of other people. You may be head of some department in an organisation, or it may be your own business or project, because, as I said in another letter, you can't achieve much by yourself alone. If you are like me you may well feel inadequately equipped for the task you have been given. After a short two years getting to know my first organisation, the Shell Company of Singapore, I was put in charge of the marketing company in Sarawak, Borneo, a country the size of Wales with rivers instead of roads. There was no telephone line to the office in Singapore, no one visited, mail took four days at least. I was on my own with three airfields and two depots to look after with a local staff of thirty-five people without even a handbook. I later discovered that this was the Shell way of grooming its future leaders – throw them in at the deep end of a small outfit where they could not do much harm but might make a difference and would certainly learn a lot.

It worked. I did learn a lot, mostly by making mistakes that I was able to correct before anyone found out. But at first I felt naked and longed for the handbook of so-called management. I now know that there isn't one. Any that you may come across, including one that I wrote myself, will turn out to be practical common sense dressed up with long words to make it seem professional. I would only urge you to remember the three different activities of Organising, Leading and Managing, and to apply them appropriately, because I truly believe that managing people, instead of leading them, is wrong and has resulted in too many dysfunctional and unhappy workplaces. You are more than a human resource.

LETTER 12

YOU AND SOCIETY

WHEN THE ISRAELITES in the Bible were getting out of control on their journey from Egypt, Moses, their leader, went up Mount Sinai and came down with two tablets on which were written ten commandments, given to him, he said, by God. These were to be the rules for their community. It was important that they had God's imprimatur because otherwise no one might have felt obliged to obey them. All rules, in short, need a higher and accepted authority. The first batch of commandments are there to reinforce the authority of the one and only God: no other gods are allowed, no graven images or idolatry. Next comes an injunction to honour your father and mother. Make no mistake, this is a hierarchical society, one in which everyone knows who calls the shots, who lays down the rules. Moses well understood that a society cannot function without rules. It is the same today. We need rules to guide our behaviour, to know what is acceptable and what is not. When those rules are officially approved by an assembly of the people, they become laws of the society and can be legally enforced.

Even smaller groups like businesses and families need rules to establish what behaviour is allowed or not. Institutions also set their own set of procedures and authorities and if you want to join them or buy from them, you are asked to conform to their processes. These don't have the force of law, but rely on an assumed contract, that by joining you are accepting their rules. The rules, be they of a business or a school or a family, are often created more for the convenience of the organisation than their customers or users. The new digital world is making it easier for the organisation to impose its discipline on all its users and employees. The digital dimension carries another advantage for the organisation, if not for the user; you cannot process and order anything digital without giving away a bunch of your personal data – your name, email and even your date of birth – none of which were necessary if you just wanted to buy their product. The technology carries its own authority; if you don't go along with their rules you cannot complete your purchase.

My wife took the view that most rules were unnecessary and could be ignored. When asked for her name and address she might fill in bogus names and details as a small way of protesting against what she saw as a form of theft, the organisation getting our data without our realising what we were giving away. Rules, she felt, had to be challenged: so many were unnecessary or weighted too much in favour of the organisation. Most regulations, to her, were not fixed tracks like railways but more like road maps – guides not rails. Driving in Italy I once remarked to an Italian friend that drivers took little notice of the speed limits. 'Oh,' he said, 'they regard them as advisory only, but if you have an accident your speed will be taken into account.' Laws as advisory not compulsory. I suspect that is the way many regard the ever-increasing list of bureaucratic rules that have encrusted modern society.

You can, of course, go to the other extreme, lie back and do what you are told. I call that submission to the rule of the invisible 'they' who are the authority. Who are they? That is the problem. We once employed a cleaning lady who was married to a soldier in the British army. One day she told me, with some pride, that the army would be giving them a new house to live in because he had been promoted to corporal. 'Where is it?' I asked. 'And when do you move?' 'They haven't told me yet,' she said. 'Who are "they"?' I asked. She looked at me as if I was stupid. 'They haven't told me yet who "they" are, have they?' Then there was the taxi when we were caught in a horrendous traffic jam: 'They ought to do something about this,' the taxi driver said angrily. Again I asked, 'Who are "they"?' 'Haven't a clue,' he said.

The invisible 'they' is usually a higher authority, often a branch of government. If we can delegate our problem upwards, to let some authority decide, we are, we like to think, free of responsibility. It seems the easy way to live, just to do what 'they' arrange or decide for you. But be careful. You can't guarantee that they will have your best interests at heart. They will want what is simplest, cheapest and most efficient for them, not for you. They will create rules and regulations that allow few exceptions, building an organised society that treats its citizens as pawns on a chess-board. This is the downside of the welfare state, a managed society with little room for individual difference. It is all done with the best intentions, no doubt, in an attempt to create a safer and more secure world for the citizens. A risk-free society, however, means a society where experiments are thought foolhardy so are never attempted. 'Is it allowed?' my children used to say when my wife suggested some new adventure. 'I have no idea,' she would reply. 'Let's see if they stop us, shall we?' I hope that you will bear these words in mind because without experiment nothing will ever change.

I used to assume that those in authority were wiser and knew better. It would be sensible therefore to let them decide many things for us. The time came, however, when I realised that some of those people had once been my students. I knew them. They were ordinary folk, doing their best for their masters and for us. They were not all-wise; like most of us they often found it easier to go along with policies that they had doubts about because they did not feel sufficient unease to blow a whistle and ruin their career. We should not rubbish the experts but should recognise that they are working within a system which they are bound by their contracts to respect. I am constantly surprised and appalled at how few of those who govern us are prepared to stand up and be counted for what they believe to be right if it puts their careers at risk. How sad it must be to live a lie just because it is easier that way. I hope that you will always follow the advice of Polonius to his son Laertes in Shakespeare's *Hamlet*: 'To thine own self be true ... Thou canst not then be false to any man.'

The upward delegation of responsibility to some invisible 'they' has another unforeseen consequence. In a regulated society anything that is not expressly regulated or forbidden is often assumed to be permitted. As one example, global businesses routinely direct their profits to those countries where taxes are lower. When anyone protests that they should pay their taxes where they make their money, the businesses reply that if that's what they want they should change their laws. Morality then is effectively defined as keeping within the law. That is a very low definition of morality, one that ends up with a cynical and calculating society. It also leads to an ever-increasing flow of new laws if we cannot rely on people to behave decently to one another. If people suffer from our actions, but we have broken no law, then it is assumed that it is up to others, often the government, to pick up the pieces or to pass new laws to prevent it happening again. No need for us to repair the damage or take responsibility. The result is a deluge of new laws and regulations, all intended to keep us safe. These rules, however, inevitably stifle initiative and creativity, unless you count as creativity the fevered search for new ways round the rules.

I would like you to remember that you have some responsibility for whoever 'they' are and what their authority is. You are not a pawn, you are a citizen, even if the British muddy the waters by calling you a subject. There is such a thing as society and it is made up of people like you. You live in a democracy, which means, literally, that power belongs to the *demos*, the people. We get the rulers we choose. The 'they' we complain about were ultimately chosen by us and people like us. We have a representative democracy, one in which we elect representatives to take decisions on our behalf, although occasionally this gets confused when our representatives decide to ask the whole population to decide something. (In my view referendums should be banned, as they are in Germany, except in specific circumstances, because they override the decisions of the people whom we elected to take those decisions. You can have one form of democracy or the other, but not both.)

Whichever form democracy takes it requires you to do your bit. You must vote, to begin with, otherwise you have no right to complain about the 'they'. In Australia voting is compulsory by law. In Britain it is voluntary. If it is raining or snowing on polling day you may decide it is too much bother to go out to vote. That is wrong. Why should the weather influence the choice of our rulers? More than voting, however, you can even be one of those elected decision-makers yourself. Democracy has many layers, starting with your own community. It is an interesting and useful thing to stand for election to your own parish council as my wife did. And why stop there? There are ever-higher levels where you can serve your country. Perhaps you could start by standing for your school or college council, becoming in a small way one of the 'they'. You might become more sympathetic to their problems.

Citizenship, however, is about more than elections. If you care about any of the big issues in society you must do more than mutter and complain to your friends. Do something about it. One friend took it upon herself to round up over 200 large organisations, who all agreed to support her campaign not only to make domestic abuse illegal but to encourage all to view it as immoral and damaging to everyone involved. The organisations all agreed to take the matter to their workforces and persuade them to take it seriously. No one asked her to do this. She was doing her duty as a citizen. Even the old gentleman I see on the common picking up litter is being a good citizen. If only more people took their citizenship seriously we would have less need of those irritating regulations. If you worry about climate change you cannot leave it all to governments. You must do your bit too: use public transport wherever possible; only eat meat once a week, if that; persuade others to follow your example; above all, vote.

I would go further. We need to apply the idea of subsidiarity in our daily lives. This ugly word has long been a part of Catholic ethical teaching and was the cornerstone of the

European Union, even if it was observed more in theory than in practice. The principle of subsidiarity is that responsibility should always reside at the lowest practical point. It favours maximum delegation or, more correctly, it favours reverse delegation, upwards. In other words, the state should not tell families how to bring up their children, although it may offer advice, but nor can families decide where the state should spend its money, even though they may well have ideas. Anything that families cannot decide on their own should be referred up to a higher authority, but that upward delegation is at the discretion of the lower body. The real power in society should lie with the citizens who delegate upwards what they cannot do for themselves. Sadly that power has been stolen from us. We need to pull it back. Subsidiarity means that you should not wait for someone to tell you what to do – just get on with it.

LETTER 13

LIFE'S CHANGING CURVES

I HAVE BORED too many audiences with my story of the road to Davy's Bar, but it meant so much to me at the time that I have to share it with you as well. It is a true story. I was driving to Avoca, a small town in Ireland. The road went through the Wicklow Mountains, a beautiful but empty area of hills and woods and lakes. I wasn't too sure of the road so when I saw someone walking his dog by the roadside I pulled up and asked him if I was on the right road to Avoca.

'Indeed you are. Keep right up this long hill, then, when you get to the top, look down into the little dip beyond. You will see a small stream, a bridge across it and Davy's Bar on the other side. You can't miss that; it's painted bright red. Have you got that?' he asked me.

'Yes,' I said. 'Up this long hill, down the dip to the small stream and Davy's Bar.'

'Great,' he said. 'Well, one kilometre before you get there turn right up the hill and you're on your way.'

It sounded so sensible, the way he said it, that I had driven off before I realised it was one of those legendary Irish directions, like 'I wouldn't start from here'. But I drove off and, sure enough, when I got to the top of the hill I could see Davy's Bar down below. I drove on keeping a lookout for that road to the right. I never saw it. I got to Davy's without passing any road. Damn that fellow, I thought as I turned round to go back up the hill. I found the road then, the other side of the hill. My helpful guide had failed to tell me that the road to the right that I needed came *before* I got to the top and before I could see Davy's Bar.

What, you may ask, has that got to do with anything? Well, it set me thinking and I realised that it was a parable about life and change.

Life, it seems to me, is a like a long S curve, lying on its side. Like this:

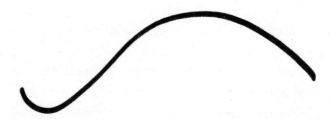

Your life, every life, even the life of a business or a school, or a political party or even a country, starts off by putting more in, by way of education, investment or experiment, before it gets going. The S curve goes down before it starts to go up. But go up, one hopes, it soon does, and goes on up, growing all the time. Nevertheless, it is an S curve and eventually the life or the organisation reaches the top and starts to go down. Well, that's life, people say, nothing lasts forever. That may be true but there could be more than one life before the end. You could start a new S curve before the first one ended, and another one after that. You can and probably should if you want to prolong your success. But that new curve is also an S curve. It dips down at first. It needs new investment, education and experiment before it starts to grow. It would be best, therefore, if it got started and out of its initial dip before the first curve peaked, because it is hard to start something new when everything is going downhill. It should look like this:

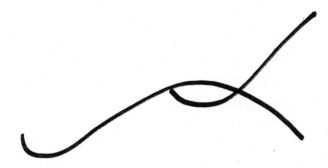

This is where the Davy's Bar story becomes relevant. You have to find the next curve while you are still climbing and before you can see the end point of the first curve. Most people cannot summon up the will to change direction until they see the writing on the wall. But by then it is often too late. They are running out of energy and resources, can't think of how to be different or how to change before they collapse. I have seen too many individuals and organisations – yes, and even countries – sitting in Davy's Bar, at the end of their road, wondering how it all went wrong, why they didn't change when times were good, why they missed the opportunity when everything was going so well and they thought it would last forever.

Psychologically it is very hard to leave a party while it is still at its height and you are enjoying it. How do you know, anyway, when you are getting near the top? It's a paradox. As

I said above, the only time you can see that point on the first curve is when you are past it, like myself on my road to Avoca. The trouble is that in life you cannot do what I did: turn round and go back. That's why you need help. It is easier for an outsider to sense the point where a new curve is needed. Every driver needs a navigator, but in this case there is no Satnav to do it for you. Only a human can do it.

Alex Ferguson, the legendary manager of Manchester United football club, skilfully spotted the point when his key players were nearing their peak so was able to sell them on before their performances fell away. But he was less perceptive when it came to himself. He left the club at its peak, leaving his successor the unenviable task of managing the decline. Terry Leahy, the chief executive of Tesco, another legend in his time, did the same at Tesco. At a personal level, too many people have stayed in their jobs too long and then found it hard to start a new career. Many who are made redundant say that they wished they had gone voluntarily years before. In my own life, my friendly adviser was my wife. Twice she suggested to me that the time was ripe for a change. Each time I resisted. Each time she was right. Each time it took me at least two years to get up to speed in my new curve, but each time it was very much worth it in the end.

Ideally, you should keep the first curve going while you begin the task of creating the next one. Organisations do it by setting up pilot projects with new and often younger people who are not so committed to the old ways. I often suggest to individuals that some form of sabbatical, a temporary break from their current work, is one way to at least explore new possibilities. But paid sabbaticals are still, unfortunately, too rare in organisations so you may have to create your own breaks as far as you can.

If you do not have a friendly adviser there are some warning signs to watch out for. Complacency is the first. When you feel that you have everything under control and have no concerns about your ability to manage whatever comes up, then beware, you may be too sure of the future for your own good. To be confident is good; to have no doubt or anxiety is dangerous. The second warning sign is a lack of curiosity about anything outside your current occupation. When my wife told me that I had become the most boring man she knew because I had become so immersed in my work that I could think of nothing else, then I knew, deep down, that it was time to lift my head up and look around me or I might be missing my way to the future Davy's Bar again.

The next question, of course, is what that new road or new curve should be. At this point it is good, I found, to start dreaming. At one stage I listed all the things that mattered in my life: money, time, place, personal satisfaction, sense of contribution and, lastly, feasibility. I then came up with three possible scenarios that I rated against these criteria. It became an agenda for long discussions with my nearest and dearest as well as some friendly outsiders. The process also opened my eyes to new possibilities so that I was ready to jump when the opportunity occurred. As I used to tell my students, stuff happens in life, apples fall unexpectedly into your lap, but it helps if you are standing in the orchard. In short, if you know the sort of thing you want you should start frequenting that world in some way, meeting people, reading relevant literature, attending conferences or visiting internet sites.

Remember too that the start of the new curve will cost more than it produces at first. In each of the three new curves that I started I had to face a big cut in pay for a few years. If, therefore, you have not been able to keep your first curve going while you explore the next, then you would be well advised to build up a reserve to see you through. The nine-month executive programme that I once instituted and ran for mid-career executives was a sabbatical experience that allowed them the time to reflect on their future along with education that might help. It was expensive but important enough to some that they were prepared to take out a loan to finance it. Others had savings. Some had persuaded their organisations to finance them as a form of leaving gratuity because it was clear that they would not be returning. This type of programmed sabbatical is not open to many but there is nothing to stop you arranging your own, provided you have saved up for it while the going was good.

Life is long. There is time for at least three different lives, maybe more. It would be a waste not to experience them. Remember only to give Davy's Bar a miss. Arrive there and you have left it too late. All you can do is to drown your sorrows and wonder how it might have been.

LETTER 14

ENOUGH IS AS GOOD AS A FEAST

IT IS AN interesting question: Why do we work so hard if we don't need to? In 1930 John Maynard Keynes, the great economist, suggested that for his grandchildren the economic problem would be solved, by which he meant that there would be no more scarcity. Technological and productivity advances would create an economic utopia in which nobody would have to work more than fifteen hours a week; we would all, if everything was fairly distributed, have enough. That worried him because, he said, we have been expressly evolved by nature – with all our impulses and deepest instincts – for the purpose of solving the economic problem. If the economic problem is solved, mankind will be deprived of its traditional purpose. We won't, in other words, know what to do with ourselves if we no longer have to work all the hours in the week to support ourselves.

Keynes was right, but only in theory. We should have solved the economic problem long ago, at least in the rich world that I live in. If we distributed things a bit more fairly no one in modern society should be in poverty or lack what they need for a decent life. As it is, the idea that enough is a good as a feast competes with the other slogan that you can never have enough of a good thing – and the latter often wins.

When it comes to money the winners take all, leaving slim pickings for those at the rear. Currently, in Britain, over half the population receives some sort of benefit from the state. In many countries governments have been forced to pay in-work benefits to provide even those in work with enough to live on. To those recipients to talk of enough being as good as a feast would be an insult. Nor are the middle classes exempt. The children of my friends, only a few years ahead of you, worry about the cost of housing, repaying their student debt, affording a pension, finding a decent job, and can only wish for enough, let alone more than enough. Keynes's forecast has not yet come true. More people are working more hours than ever before even though they already probably have enough to lead a reasonably comfortable life. Why do we do it? Is it to buy more stuff, or to show how important we are? Or because our colleagues are getting more than us? Whatever the reason we do seem to have an insatiable appetite for more: more things, more money, more entertainment, more everything. When John D. Rockefeller, the billionaire philanthropist back in the last century, was asked what 'enough' was, he said 'just one more'. Many of us seem to agree with him. There seems to be no limit to our appetites.

Part of the reason, however, must surely be that we love work: not necessarily the actual work itself but everything that goes with it. Work gives many of us our identity. We are what we do. It provides the glue of society, brings people together, shapes our day and gives us a reason to get up in the morning.

And yet, and yet. Our hunter ancestors did not have that urge. Research on the Bushmen of the Kalahari Desert showed that the idea that our prehistoric ancestors had a hard life of unremitting toil was not true. They only worked when they had to, did not store food, had few wants, which were easily satisfied. They only had to take up their spears and go hunting when more was food was needed. As a result they worked only fifteen hours a week. There would have been no point in working more. Some have called them 'the first affluent society'. The missing ingredient, however, was money. Money can be stored more easily than food and can be exchanged for a multiplicity of other things. Without money our ancestors saw no point in working longer than they had to. Had the Bushmen had money or other means of exchange their lives might have been less leisured. Perhaps the love of money really was the root of all evil.

Until I was sixty the idea of having enough money was a distant dream. I used to carry a card around with me. It had two columns, 'Money In' and 'Money Out'. It was my constant reminder that the 'out' must not exceed the 'in'. Then, having turned sixty, the kids had left home, the mortgage was paid off, my books had started to sell and I had discovered that overpaid form of performance art: talking to business conferences. Suddenly, late in life, the in column was larger than the out. Dilemma! Should I enjoy the bonanza or practise what I preach and settle for enough?

At one point I was interviewed by a journalist for *Fortune* magazine. She wondered why I restricted my big lectures to ten a year when these lectures were, at that period, earning me several thousand pounds a time. 'Could you do more?' she asked me. 'Do you ever turn down invitations to speak?'

'Yes,' I said. 'Often. These lectures can involve too much travelling and take me away from my home and my writing, so why would I want to do more? As it is they provide me with quite enough money to support my family and meet my needs.'

'But you could make so much more money, so aren't you tempted?'

'What would I do with that extra money, if I don't need it?'

She thought for a moment; then she said, 'You could collect things.'

It was an eye-opener. She was right. Rich people use their unnecessary wealth to collect things: houses, yachts, art, even friends and wives. These are their trophies, the visible signs of their success. Just as the emperors of Ancient Rome would herald their successful military campaigns with processions of captured chieftains and treasures in ceremonial marches through the capital, so our modern emperors have to have their own trophies to display.

My wife and I, however, were not collectors. We tried from that point on to make the idea of 'enough' one of the rules of our life. Each year, during my working career, we would calculate how many money-making contracts to speak or teach or write I needed to undertake in order to make sure that we would have enough; enough, that is, to enable us to live relatively comfortable lives. We soon realised that the lower we set the bar for enough the more freedom we had to do all the other things. Blessed are the poor, you could say, provided always that you are poor by choice and not necessity.

Keynes believed that mankind was bred to work and would be lost without the financial need to do so. That, however, is to take a very narrow view of work. Along with many others, I have found that the work I do for free is much more satisfying that the work I do or did for money to support my family. By work for free I include not only work for charities or good causes, but also the work I do at home: cooking, entertaining, caring for children – including you – fixing things that go wrong. I love cooking but after a day at the chopping board I know that it is work as well as pleasure. We also ran an informal counselling service in which we invited anyone who wanted to talk about their life or work to come to breakfast in our London apartment for free. We hoped it helped those who came. We enjoyed it, but it was work, with all the effort and time we put into it, but we also appreciated the satisfaction that work can bring. Keynes was too pessimistic. There will always be good things for idle hands and minds to do, as Keynes must have known, for his own life was full of unpaid but worthwhile work. I might even say that of this sort of work there can never be enough.

The idea of enough is not confined to money and work. It works in every part of life. Food and drink, most obviously, where enough is literally as good as a feast. There is also the temptation to concentrate on some subject or activity to the exclusion of anything else. That runs the risk of what economists call opportunity cost, when you miss out on the opportunity of developing an alternative interest or activity. One year, when I was totally absorbed in my work, my wife told me that I had become the most boring man she knew. By ignoring the rule of enough I had narrowed my life and might have ruined my marriage.

LETTER 15

IT'S THE ECONOMY, STUPID

THIS WAS THE phrase that James Carville, Bill Clinton's campaign manager, insisted was the key message of the 1992 election campaign. He was concerned about the loss of jobs and the plight of low-level workers at that time in America, about the dollars in their pockets or the lack of them. It is a reminder to me that economics is both important and too little discussed, in schools or in homes, when you are young. Don't worry – this is not going to be a discourse on the future of the British economy or a lecture on Maynard Keynes, Britain's most illustrious economist, although he is well worth studying. No, I am concerned with your personal economy, your money. I agree that this is getting a bit more basic than the more philosophical tone of my other letters but money matters. It matters most when you don't have it and it can matter too much when you have more of it. What follows is what I have learnt from my own experience.

I grew up, as I have told you, in a vicarage in Ireland. Money was never mentioned at home even though there was never much of it. This was because of the way my father, and his profession, thought about the problem of financing his calling. The Church of Ireland, his employer, did not want him to see money as in any way a reward for his work. That would have meant measuring his success or failure, and how do you measure his 'care of souls' as it was called? So they gave him accommodation and a stipend. The stipend was designed to be enough to live on but not to get rich on. It was barely enough but it was sufficient, given that it was accompanied by a free house and large garden. This arrangement meant that money was never the measure of anything my father did. He was free to dedicate himself to his work without worrying about his pay because that was fixed, take it or leave it. Moderate income was the norm of the profession. You did not join it to get rich. More professions might usefully adopt the stipendiary principle. Or you might think of applying it yourself in your own life.

The real truth is that when you are doing something that you really care about, the money, or lack of it, does not matter that much. Painters will live in an attic if they have to. In my own career I moved from oil executive to academic to freelance author, in each case looking for more enjoyment and fulfilment in my work but having to accept a downward curve in my finances. As long as there was enough, my wife and I were content. I am not suggesting that you aim to follow such a downward financial spiral as I did, but I am stressing that it is more important that you enjoy what you are doing than what you are earning. To do that you may have to adjust your living standards to your income rather than the other way round. Not easy, if your friends have higher standards than you, but worthwhile in the end. Fighting for money is soul-destroying.

My wife had a strange but very important philosophy about money. She distinguished between investments and expenditure. If something was an investment she went for the best and would borrow if need be to achieve it. I remember discussing her plans for a ping-pong shed in our garden. I overheard the builder asking, 'Do you want it in ply or oak?' My heart sank as I heard her say, 'Oak, of course.' But she was right in the end because it now also serves as a very useful spare bedroom. Cameras, of course, for her as a photographer, were always an investment, no matter how ludicrously expensive. 'You could buy a car for that,' I said once, to which she just replied, 'I don't need a car, I need a camera.' When it came to expenditure it was a different matter. She hated spending money if she did not have to. Eating in restaurants was ridiculously expensive compared with cooking the same meal at home, and much more noisy. Taxis were out when buses for we oldies were free. Good clothes, however, were an investment, provided that they would last for years.

I was the reverse. Having grown up in the culture of enough, where make do and mend was the motto as opposed to throw away and start anew, I hankered after the chance to indulge myself in spending on experiences rather than things: eating out, theatres, travel and so on, things where there would be nothing to show for the money. Fortunately I was married to someone who thought exactly the opposite. All this is to underline how wise, in retrospect, I thought my wife was, although it took many years for some of her investments to bear fruit. I can now recommend her philosophy as a good way to live with enough. It is also the best way to run the national economy too. Borrow only for investment; spend within your income. My wife would have made a good Chancellor of the Exchequer.

All this is by way of emphasising that money and fulfilment are uneasy bedfellows. I had long ago realised that my early dream of finding work that I loved doing, with agreeable companions and adequate money, was just that: a dream. Few will find that unlikely combination, although if you have a professional vocation you are in with a chance. I eventually stopped searching for that elusive perfect job and realised that I had to combine two or three different types of work, what I called a work portfolio, to get the right combination of money, enjoyment and fulfilment. I discovered that my confer-ence talks were, eventually, enough by themselves to cover my cost of living. My real work, I insisted, was my books, even if they did not sell. I called it a three-part work portfolio, a word that came to be increasingly popular in the changing world of work.

I recommend the portfolio idea to you if, like me, you can't find the ideal job. Find something that you can do for money for part of your time, leaving enough space to do what you really want to do. Just be careful that you do not get too seduced by the money bit. Life is too precious to waste it on making money.

LETTER 16

'WE' BEATS 'I' ALL THE TIME

I HOPE THAT you will be lucky enough to go through life saying 'we' more often than 'I'. Companionship is so important, to have someone with whom you can share your hopes and uncertainties. It does not have to be a life partner. It can be your family, a work group or a whole organisation, even a movement. In another letter I mentioned Robin Dunbar's idea that you can have a maximum of five best friends and fifteen good friends. These will be the most important 'we' in your life. These people, particularly the first five, will be your anchors in life, keeping you upright when life seems to be falling around you. These few know you too well to be deceived by your false ambitions. You can be completely honest with them. You are walking life together, so bond them to you tightly and treat them kindly.

Friendship has been cherished down the ages. Shakespeare famously has Polonius give this advice to his son Laertes in *Hamlet*:

Those friends thou hast, and their adoption tried,
Grapple them to thy soul with hoops of steel;
But do not dull thy palm with entertainment
Of each new-hatch'd, unfledged comrade.

Francis Bacon said that without true friends the world is but a wilderness. He went on:

> The light that a man receiveth by counsel from another is drier and purer than that which cometh from his own understanding ... [for] a man cannot speak to his son but as a father; to his wife but as a husband; to his enemy but upon terms: whereas a friend may speak as the case requires ...

I must apologise on his behalf for his concentration on the male. He was a creature of his time and I'm sure now that he would say the same of a woman. A true friend will speak truth to you, even when it hurts. I used to comb my hair to conceal my increasing baldness. I looked ridiculous. No one said anything, neither my wife nor my kids. Finally, a friend told me to own up. 'You are bald,' she said, 'don't try to pretend you are not.' That truth really did set me free, once I had accepted it.

If you are lucky you may discover an older friend who will become your guide and mentor for part of your life, someone who has spotted the best in you and wants to encourage it. In my own experience there have been three people who have helped me over the threshold of a new life: a schoolmaster who made sure I went to university; a boss who had such confidence in me that he promoted me to a full professorship before I had done enough to deserve it ('You will have to justify my decision after the appointment,' he said); and another who introduced me to America. I owe to them a large chunk of my life and will always be grateful. The Hindu philosophy would say that I can best repay them by doing the same service to others. This I now try to do.

Most of your close friends, however, will be of the same age and sex because they are those who are most likely to have shared some life-shaping experience with you. The bonds are created by shared experiences. You may have shared rooms at university, been in the same team, climbed mountains linked to each other, depended on each other in some way that pulled you together. It took me a long while to have a friendship with a woman without the idea of sex being there in the background because that was the only experience we might have shared, although it was seldom life-shaping or long-lasting. Later I found that my sex-free friendships with women were often the most rewarding because they helped me to look at the world from very different angles.

My wife was definitely my best friend. Did it help that we were married? Of course – this was the life-shaping experience we shared for fifty-five years. There was also something reassuring in the thought that we were bonded together by law and a public commitment. More than that, however, our lives were bonded together by a shared commitment, to each other and to our children and, later, to our grandchildren. Without that shared commitment it would not have worked. Of course, there is also love, but love, once the passion dies away, is the physical and emotional expression of togetherness, of the 'we'. One of my people-watching games is to count the number of 'I's and 'we's someone uses in their conversation. You learn a lot about people by listening.

What people don't tell you, however, is that to enjoy the undoubted benefits of 'we' in any relationship, be it a partnership, a close friendship or a work group, you have to first invest in it. There can be no free ride in a true togetherness. To get you first have to give, and you can only give if you care, and, ideally, care more for the other than yourself. The poet Philip Larkin put it well:

> We should be careful
> Of each other, we should be kind
> While there is still time.

Kindness is the glue of friendship. You can argue with a friend, disagree with their political or religious views, as long as you do it kindly, respecting their right to disagree with you. As I mentioned before, the Scottish philosopher David Hume said that truth proceeds from arguments between friends. He was right. I have learnt so much from my arguments with my friends, often surprising myself with what I come out with; 'How do I know what I think until I hear what I say,' the Irishman said. It's the same in marriage; the best marriages are often a blend of complementary but different contributions, as was ours. The new freedom for couples to go beyond the stereotyped roles of husband and wife and explore new combinations can often lead to a better togetherness.

We used to divide our friends into two groups: the drains and the radiators. Drains sap your energy, leaving you wondering when they will leave. The radiators are the ones who, when we meet, enrich our lives with their conversation, their ideas and their energy. It's a bit unfair since even the most boring of drains can come alive if we are able to find a topic that interests them or even if we just choose to focus on them and their concerns for a while. Get people to smile and their whole face lights up. More crucially our little game was a way of reminding ourselves to be more radiator than drain in our own friendships. Mostly, I discovered, it is a matter of energy, how much of it I was prepared to invest in a person or a situation. Occasionally, with family for instance, it was tempting to relax, opt out or just coast along with the conversation. Then I would pull myself up short. Why was I being so disrespectful to my nearest and dearest, taking their interest in me for granted? Radiators are always welcome; drains are tolerated at best.

The 'we' carries over into the workplace, even when it isn't an actual place. When I did a study of entrepreneurs they all agreed that they could not have done it on their own, even if they were the ones who had the original idea. I have already argued that small is best but for small to work the groups have to be teams. Teams are groups with a shared purpose in which each member has their own individual contribution to make. They are a looser form of friendship but function best when there is a real commitment to a shared purpose and a respect for each other's contribution.

The best illustration that I can give you of how a team should work is provided by a rowing eight on the river. There are eight people in the boat, or in fact nine if you include the cox. The interesting thing about the boat is how the leadership changes as the task changes. There is no one leader, something that other organisations might note. There is, it is true, the captain of the boat. He or she is the official leader, largely responsible for representing the crew to the world as well as choosing the members. He or she is, however, only the first among equals once the boat is on the river, often rowing in the middle of the boat. The leadership task then devolves on to the stroke, who sets the pace for the others. But there is also the cox, the one person who is in the boat but does not row. He or she is, however, the only person who can see where they are going and therefore is responsible for steering the boat. There is then one more person: the coach. He or she isn't in the boat at all but gives advice from the bank or in briefing sessions before or after.

The rowing eight is, in my view, the ideal model for a team. Individuals are chosen for their individual contribution but have to work closely together or the whole does not work. Some years ago Oxford recruited a team of international rowers, who happened to be studying at the university, to make up the crew in the traditional boat race against Cambridge. These international stars felt no need to join the rest of the group for early-morning training. They were the experts, kindly lending their talents to the team. It did not work; eight self-described stars do not a team make. They would have had to subordinate their egos to the group effort for it to work. They were dropped from the team shortly before the race and a younger, less experienced crew selected. The new crew made up in their dedication and commitment for what they lacked in individual talent or experience. They won the race, proving that 'we' beats 'I' if 'we' are a team.

It is the same in the arts and in other team sports. The actor or musician or player who attempts to steal the show will not only ruin the show but also his or her own reputation. Tennis players, however good they are, will build a team around them and even the best will have a coach. No one is too good not to need to learn. Other organisations should take heed. Small groups, changing leadership, a common focus and a clear objective: it is a recipe for excellence. Note, too, the role of the outside coach and the regular briefing sessions. No one is so good that they have no need of an outside perspective, nor should any activity go without regular reviews. It is a comradeship based on trust and shared interests. If you find yourself in such a group you will be fortunate. Later on, given the chance and the responsibility, you would be wise to make every effort to create rowing eight type groups.

My wife died recently. For the first time in over half a century I am on my own. It feels very strange. I can't say I'm lonely because I have many people who come to see me, invite me out, go to theatres or concerts with me, but the to-getherness has gone, the sense of a shared life or a common project. There is, it is true, a certain freedom; I don't have to think about the other person when I am making decisions: I can go to bed when I like, eat what I choose, see whom I like. But the freedom does not compensate for the lack of to-getherness. Of course, my wife is still around in my head. I think of her almost every moment, still doing all the things that we used to do in the way she liked. I still look across to her chair to see if she is asleep during the television news, as she used to be. I still hear her voice in my ear as I plan a trip or agree to a piece of work. I still imagine her reading this and giving me her frank opinion, for good or ill.

I have lost my best friend. Perhaps you only know how special someone or something is when you have lost it. So it is with friendship. Never take it for granted. Cherish those special friends. You will miss them if they go.

LETTER 17

WHEN TWO BECOME ONE

IT IS MY wish for you that you should, in due course, fall in love and enter a long and committed relationship, whether you call it marriage or something else. As a foundation for life and a future family there is nothing better, although, like every relationship, it won't always be easy. The best thing I can do to help is to give you the story of how it worked for me, in the hope that you can learn something from it.

It was a day laden with romance, of anxiety mixed with joy. It was my wedding day. We had made promises to each other, raised glasses, cut a cake and waved goodbye to assembled guests. We were on our way. To what? We had never sat down and talked about it, about what it would be like, who would do what and what would be the priorities. We were good together. We would go on being good together. No need to spoil it all with plans and job descriptions as if it was a business. Being fifty years ago, it was just assumed that my career would have priority, would determine where we would live and how we would live. She, Elizabeth, would have the main responsibility for the home, and for the children when and if they came. Whatever interests and talents she would develop, and there were to be many, would have to be fitted into her domestic priorities and my life. I assumed that she thought so too. I don't remember asking her.

Looking back, it was incredibly selfish of me, particularly as my career took me into ever more absorbing areas, from business to academia to working for the Church. What added to the problem was that each job came with less, not more, remuneration than the last. That left Elizabeth to fill the growing financial gap, which she always and valiantly did, running her own interior design business and later leasing and letting out a succession of small apartments, all whilst still managing the home front. As one result, I never gave her any money to buy food or household necessities. She took care of all those out of her earnings, leaving me to look after the regular outgoings: the mortgage, the utilities, the repairs and, of course, the booze. That was unusual. My father had given my mother a regular monthly allowance, which she was expected to account for. I remember her agonising over her accounts, trying to remember what she had spent on what. A frequent item seemed to be SPG, which I took to stand for the Society for the Propagation of the Gospel, a missionary charity dear to my parents' hearts, until my mother confessed one day that it stood for Something Probably Grub!

In that respect we had moved on, or society had. I was not the boss in the home, even if I was still the main anchor of our lives outside it. Yet, once again, we never formally negotiated these arrangements. They just emerged as circumstances dictated. I am ashamed, now, at how little I contributed to the domestic scene, leaving early in the morning in our only car, returning late in the evening after the children had gone to bed, letting my wife take the children to school on her bicycle, to do all the shopping and housework and still find time for her work. But we were both the children of our time and that was the widely understood pattern of marriage among our friends and colleagues.

Why did we not discuss it more formally, I wonder? We had made that set of vows and promises to each other in front of a bunch of our friends and relatives, a contract to love and care for each other, but the detailed specifics of what and how had never been spelt out. The necessary appendix to the formal contract had been omitted. Like almost everyone else, we made it up as we went along. As we did so, we began to realise that we each had different notions of what that appendix should contain. Because we had never spoken these thoughts out loud, mutual resentments smouldered and occasionally flared up.

The truth is that every relationship is based around an implicit contract, a balance of expectations. Unless these are made clear, misunderstandings are inevitable. Moreover, the contracts need to be fair to each party. Many years earlier, in the course of my business career, I had to negotiate a contract with a Chinese agent in Malaysia. We agreed the terms, shook hands and shared the traditional glass of brandy. I then took out the official company contract form for him to sign. He was indignant. 'What is that for?' he said angrily. 'Don't you trust me? The contract will only work if both of us get what we want out if it. A signature should be unnecessary. In fact, it makes me suspect that you think you have got a better deal than me and want to lock me into it.' I persuaded him that it was only a company formality, but I took his point. I have never forgotten it. If both parties don't feel the deal is fair it won't stick, in business or in relationships. We would have avoided much unhappiness had I remembered my Chinese contract experience, if I had made a series of deals as we went through life, deals that gave both of us enough of what we wanted to ensure that the contract worked. That original Chinese contract was also time limited. It had to be renegotiated in due course. So it is with those implicit marriage contracts. Circumstances change. Jobs change. Kids grow up. People die or fall ill.

So it was for us. When I was fifty I ran out of jobs. There were none that I wanted that might want me. Too young and too poor to retire, I became a self-employed writer and lecturer. The freedom was exciting but the income precarious and I found it embarrassing to ask for it. My wife came to the rescue. She became my agent and business manager and was very good at it. So good, in fact, that I got both busier and richer. Until the day when she in effect gave in her notice. Her life, she said, had become submerged in mine. She had recently graduated with a degree in photography after five years of part-time study, and now wanted to fulfil her dream of becoming a professional portrait photographer. My wife was now on her way, even if it had taken her most of the first fifty years of her life to get there. Largely my fault, of course.

This time we did sit down to a proper contract negotiation. We agreed to split the year in two. For the six summer months her work would have priority in our diary, with mine providing some background support. I would concentrate on research and writing and take on no outside commitments. The winter months would be free for my speaking engagements, with her help in organising them. Furthermore we decided to split the cooking and catering, with each doing half, she in our London apartment, I in the country cottage. We were fortunate in that we were both independent workers, the children had left home and we were free to organise our lives as we saw fit.

Not everyone has that degree of freedom, but most couples do need to rearrange their relationship in mid-life as their circumstances change, when children go or work dries up or changes. Too often one party makes a unilateral decision to change the contract without discussion, even in some situations to look for another partner altogether, often someone with whom they have worked. We were lucky. We were able to help each other and to share our work, and that brought us together in a new relationship.

That contract lasted for over twenty years. They were fruitful and enjoyable times. Then circumstances changed again. I was approaching seventy-five, a time when I was required by law to convert my savings into an annuity. That meant that I did not need to earn as much as in the past. I had a pension of sorts. At the same time our children belatedly began to produce grandchildren. I had not realised how rewarding, but also how time-consuming, these little people can be. Clearly, life had to change once more. This time it was going to be more like what people think of as retirement, in that paid work no longer dominated our two lives, but retiring was not how it felt. We were busier than ever, but differently. A new contract was needed.

Work, of some sort, had to be part of it. Life without something serious to do seems pointless. Since we no longer needed so much moneymaking work we could afford to do more voluntary work. We began to combine our skills and interests on a number of joint pro bono projects, making photo documentaries for voluntary organisations. No longer did we split the year in two because we now worked together. Living now on a fixed and probably declining income we also needed to simplify our way of life, downsizing and discarding instead of accumulating. So much that we had once done now seemed unnecessary, even pointless. Life moves on and leaves a lot behind. It was important, therefore, that we took time to reflect on how best to use the remaining years in our life, now that ambition was pointless and achievement meant something different than worldly success. These last years are precious years and we needed to make the most of them. The new contract needed careful thought. There is a saying that happiness is having something to work on, someone to love and something to hope for. These three ingredients are, to us, what made life worth living.

Of course, we are the fortunate members of a fortunate generation. Many will envy the apparent ease of our lives, although it did not seem easy at the time. Not everyone will have the freedom to make the choices we did. But whatever our circumstances we all have choices. If we are lucky enough to be in a relationship those choices have to take account of the other person. And they need constant revision as our lives change. Otherwise they won't work. We learnt that the long way, often the hard way. But it was worth it. I sometimes say, half seriously, when others are talking of their second or third marriages, that I, too, was on my third marriage. But, in my case, they were to the same woman, and that made all the difference. Try it, when the time comes. Stay the same but different.

LETTER 18

WHAT YOU CAN'T COUNT MATTERS
MORE THAN WHAT YOU CAN

WHAT ISN'T COUNTED doesn't count. That is how the saying goes and it is true that much of life is a numbers game. From the size of the economy to your consumption of electricity or the nourishment in your diet, it is numbers that are the measure. Numbers, and the science of numbers, mathematics and statistics, are the only language apart from music that is truly international, and even music is numbers in another form. Everyone in the world can do the same sums, read the same graphs, make the same calculations, irrespective of what language they speak. That is truly remarkable. It is just one reason why everyone should learn the language of mathematics, and of statistics in particular, as early as possible.

Numbers, however, are dodgy. They don't always tell the truth, or not the whole truth. The balance sheet in the accounts of a business will not include an estimate of the value of what that business will often say are their principal assets: their people. They only get counted as a cost on the profit and loss account. The Gross National Product number of a country includes much more than production. The costs of government and the armed forces, and those incurred by a road crash and the consequent hospital and repair bills are all counted in, but hardly deserve to be seen as the output of the country. On the other hand, all unpaid work, be it child-rearing, housework or caring for elderly relatives, goes uncounted while estimates of prostitution and drug-dealing are included. Statisticians have calculated that if you had to employ people to do all the home care tasks that are needed you might have to pay each person a minimum of £25,000 year. Add that to our GNP and the nation would jump the queue, yet nothing would have changed. You can't understand numbers unless you know where they come from and what they include or exclude.

Numbers are easily manipulated. A health report might say that those who run more than four miles a day are 50 per cent more likely than others to develop some particular foot ailment. Joggers start worrying. What the report would not say is that the ailment is found in only 1 per cent of runners; 50 per cent of 1 per cent is not worth the worry. Or, to emphasise the rise or fall of a currency, journalists might draw a graph in which the starting point is not zero but something much higher and nearer the average. That very shortened graph will exaggerate any rise or fall. You have to know what you are looking at and its context.

That proved to be only too true in the Vietnam War, which was largely planned by Robert McNamara as the American Secretary of Defense. Robert McNamara was, by any standards, a wildly successful man. Harvard graduate, president of Ford Motor Company, then rising to the heights of U.S. Secretary of Defense in the 1960s. McNamara epitomised American élan and brio. But he had one major flaw – he saw the world in numbers. The problem with this method in this context was that the Vietnam War was characterised by the immeasurable chaos of human conflict and not the definable production of parts on a factory assembly line, or, in this case, the body counts of friend and foe, which was how McNamara measured success or failure. Things spun out of control as McNamara's statistical method failed to take into account numerous unseen variables, and the public turned against US involvement in the war through a cultural change that would transform the country. Although on paper America was 'winning' the war, in the end they lost it.

The sociologist Daniel Yankelovitch summed up Mc-Namara's problem in what he called the McNamara Fallacy. It goes like this:

The first step is to measure whatever can be easily measured. This is OK as far as it goes. The second step is to disregard that which can't be easily measured or to give it an arbitrary quantitative value. This is artificial and misleading. The third step is to presume that what can't be measured easily really isn't important. This is blindness. The fourth step is to say that what can't be easily measured really doesn't exist. This is suicide.

McNamara even deceived himself. Long after the war he admitted that he had often thought that the war was probably unwinnable but he still believed his numbers and fought on. Something similar happens in education. Teachers will say that they want to develop the whole child and to bring out the best in them. They also recognise that examination results only measure some aspects of any young person's abilities, yet those are the only numbers they have so those are the ones that they concentrate on and the ones by which they and their schools are judged. Any other talents or competences can't be measured so are effectively ignored. Teachers recognise this but they are driven by the numbers and the system to concentrate on those competences and skills that *can* be measured. These become the effective substitute for a full and rounded education. Parents collude because they in their turn want their children to succeed in the system, even if, like McNamara, their hunch is that the system is only telling half the truth.

As life goes on it gets worse. How do we measure our progress? Life is a journey. We need to know where we are on that journey, even if we have no particular destination in mind. We also want to be happy, to love and be loved, to enjoy friendship and the joy of companionship, to be able to travel, play sport, appreciate art, good food and great music, all the things that make life pleasurable. We may value all these things but we can't measure them. So we look for substitute measures – the number of 'likes' on Facebook or our score of Twitter followers, or, if this is important to us, we will compare job titles with our contemporaries or our salaries. In the end these numbers become important in themselves and are pursued for their own sake.

Why do business executives eagerly accept what are often grossly excessive pay bonuses, even though they know they do not need them and must also be aware of how unpopular they are? It is because they are the best public measure there is of their success. If their bonuses were paid in philanthropic gift tokens they might be just as content, as long as all bonuses were paid that way. Come to think of it, why do they need bonuses to persuade them to do their job? No other profession works that way; nor, when I first started work, did the company I worked for. Make money the definition of success and the numbers may shine so brightly in your eyes that you lose sight of the real purpose of your work or life.

The McNamara Fallacy means that much of life gets pushed down into second or third place. Beauty and harmony, love and kindness, hope and courage, honesty and loyalty: all the things that make life worth living – along with their opposites: cheating, deceit and dishonesty – get swept under the carpet. Nice guys finish last, sometimes. But that depends on how you define the race. If you know how you want to live your life you won't worry too much about the numbers. Until they catch you out.

One day a developer walked into our family home and offered to buy it for redevelopment. I said it had been our family home for twenty years and was not for sale. He replied that everyone had their price and offered me a sum three times what the house was worth. My eyes widened. What could we do with all that money? A smarter home in a better area? Two homes perhaps? 'Done,' I said after only a minute's thought, and shook hands on the deal. I went into the kitchen to tell my wife. 'I've sold our family home,' I said. 'You've done what?' she cried, outraged. 'You have no right to do that.' I told her the price. 'Oh, wow,' she said, as entranced as I was by the thought of all those numbers. Before the contract was signed we set off to look at all those enticing properties in more fashionable areas, only to discover that none of them offered all the space and convenience of our current home. We would have to give up a lot of what we liked about our rambling, comfortable and shabby home. While we were still looking, still keen to spend all that tempting loot, the economy crashed and the deal fell through. I still live in that old family home forty years later, as do, in another part of it, our daughter and her family. We shudder now to think of what might have happened if we had signed the contract before the crash. The money numbers had temporarily blinded us. As they do.

My wife and I used to play tennis every afternoon, if the weather allowed. I played to win and kept a close eye on the score. My wife couldn't care less who won or what the score was, she just loved playing the game. I maintained that without the score the game was meaningless. She thought that I was missing the point. I need numbers, money numbers and tennis scores, to know where I stand, both financially and at play. Thanks to my wife, however, I no longer make those numbers the point.

Perhaps life should be like golf. You can play for the fun of it, or you can play to win, or both. But the handicap system means that a better player has to give away more strokes to the weaker player. That makes for a fairer game. The system, however, also makes it possible for the better player to take pride in his handicap even though it penalises him in the competition. I have always thought that the handicap system in competitive sport should be copied in other walks of life because the handicap numbers encourage you to keep improving without spoiling the enjoyment of the game. I now try to think like a golfer. I like to keep the score in the different parts of my life. I also have some basic requirements, mainly financial, that, like a handicap, I try to keep as low as possible. None of those numbers, however, should detract from the fact that the game is the thing. My wife was right: playing, not winning or losing, is what matters.

To me, success has nothing much to do with things. Yes, I am pleased that I have a nice home and can afford to eat well but that isn't enough to justify a life. So what am I proud of in my life? That was the question put to me by a journalist the other day. 'Well,' I said, 'I'm quite proud of the books I have written because some people have found that they helped them, but books grow dusty and end up in the dump. I think, therefore, that I am most proud of my family and of my grandchildren because they will last. I hope that they will go on to do great things or be great people.' In other words, any success that I may have had in my life is measured by the lives of others: my family or some who have found something in my books that was useful, even though I never knew. One of the nicest letters I ever received had no address and no signature. It just said 'Thank you' on an otherwise blank piece of paper. That felt good.

LETTER 19

THE LAST QUARTER

AMAZING AS IT may seem to you now, it is quite possible that you will live to be a hundred. I suspect that this letter will not be of much interest to you now, but it raises issues that you will have to start considering in a few years' time. The last quarter of your life will be the twenty-five years from seventy-five to a hundred. Even seventy-five must seem a long way off, but my guess is that seventy-five will be the normal 'retirement' age by the time you reach it. I put 'retirement' in inverted commas because I do not believe that you would want to retire from life for the last quarter of it. Indeed, I suspect that the very word 'retirement' will be itself retired by then. This, therefore, is my reflection on what life may be like for you in those years.

'They retired me, the brutes.' This was a 66-year-old explaining why she had had to leave the job she loved before she was ready to go. Odd how for her the word 'retired' had somehow become a transitive verb, something that other people did to you, whether you wanted it or not. Now it would be illegal to force it on anyone against their will, though it frequently happens. Others, however, as they read of plans to raise the pensionable age, might think her lucky to have been able to leave so soon. Those are the ones who cannot wait to stop work, assuming that life without compulsory labour would be a time of unalloyed bliss. Some suspect, however, more realistically, that the idea of a leisured old age, financed by pensions of one sort or another, is a dwindling dream, to be enjoyed only by those privileged few at the top of corporations or, it seems, those who chose to work for most of their lives in the public sector.

The problem, we are told, is that we are living longer. Odd, again, how the gift of an extra ten years or so should be seen as a problem. Opportunities do, however, turn into problems if they are not foreseen or prepared for and this one, strangely, seems to have been creeping up on us unnoticed, perhaps because it was never going personally to affect those currently in power. As if climate change and pensions and retirement issues fall into the 'not in my lifetime' syndrome, something to leave for successors to deal with, even though in both cases it was clear that lead times of forty to fifty years were needed for any decisions to take effect.

The truth is that there is no pensions crisis or retirement problem – yet. Seventy per cent of those aged between fifty and sixty-four today are still in employment. And if this seems to leave a lot of people out of work we should remember that even in the peak of life, when we are aged thirty-five to forty-nine, only 82 per cent of us are officially employed – the rest are often also working but in the home and uncounted. The great majority of that 70 per cent in employment at present will also have a second pension building up, will own their own home and may well have inherited or expect to inherit a surplus home from their parents who were the first major home-owning generation. There will always be some who struggle, but the great majority of the new retirees in this decade will not be poor. They can expect to enter their Third

Age of 'living', after the first two of learning and working, in good shape. For them the next ten to twenty years will truly be ones of opportunity. Unfortunately it may not be the same for you unless you yourself do something about it long before.

That still leaves them, and eventually you, with the question: What do we do? But it is their successor generation and the one after that, your generation, that will have to face the first question: What will we live on? For these age groups it seems clear that despite a slightly larger and later state pension the expectation will be that they will have to be responsible themselves for providing the bulk of their post-employment income. Employers won't do it for them unless they are forced to, nor will the state compel them to save. Some will. Many won't, because the pressure of meeting today's costs leaves tomorrow's problems ignored or postponed. They may then have to go on working into their seventies, or even their eighties.

That is not necessarily a bad fate. In spite of that misused phrase 'work-life balance', work is not the opposite of life but is at its core, provided that it is work one enjoys and can be done at a pace which suits you. It would be more accurate to say what many want is not more life and less work but a better balance of the different types of work. The work we do for money needs to be complemented by the work we do for love or duty, in the home or the community, as well as by the work we do for pleasure and the work we do to improve our skills or knowledge. Ideally one needs a mix of all these types of work. The only difference that age makes is that the mix changes: more work from choice, less work for pay.

For most, the balance of the work mix will change as they move through life, with paid work diminishing as they get older but not necessarily disappearing. A farmer in his seventies, when asked what his life was like, replied, 'The same only slower.' Many would like to be able to say the same, doing what they know how to do, but only on two days a week, not five – just enough to add to their income but with time left over for their other interests. If that is their wish the world of work is moving their way.

Organisations are endlessly rearranging themselves, disgorging ever more chunks of their work, pushing many outside and hiring them back as part-timers or independents. It often makes the place more difficult to manage but they do it to increase their flexibility, and also, if the truth be told, to escape some of the obligations that legislation imposes on them. Ironically, some measures that are designed to protect the interests of the worker, for example by making it more difficult to dismiss someone, can end up deterring employers from hiring them in the first place. Already one quarter of the workforce is part-time and another quarter are self-employed or in tiny one- to four-person businesses, most of them working that way from choice but others because they have to, particularly as they age.

It is all good practice for the final quarter of life when almost all of us will find ourselves responsible for our own lives with no help from any organisation. By then we will have traded what was left of our security inside an organisation for the freedom outside. It is not a bad exchange, as many have found, provided we have a skill and know how to market it, price it and maintain it. There lies the rub. With self-initiative discouraged by our organisations we are bereft when we leave them. What we need is what independent professionals have always had: agents – people who are paid to find customers for us. It is a role that trades unions could play but choose not to. It is something that employment agencies claim to be doing but could do better. It is a role that voluntary bodies could usefully take on. Too many languish, their skills and talents unnoticed.

Unnoticed even by themselves, sometimes. One advertising executive, made redundant in his late forties, found his way to an outplacement consultant.

'What can you do?' he was asked.

'Advertising,' he replied.

'Yes, but what else, since that career has reached its likely end?'

'I can't imagine anything else I could do or be.'

'Why don't you ask a dozen people who know you well', the consultant said, 'to each list one thing you are good at and come back with the list?'

On his return he confessed that he had been amazed at the list of qualities they saw in him. 'But it's odd,' he said, 'none of them mentioned advertising.'

Our past can blind us to our future.

In the new fast-changing world potential counts for more than past experience and the ability to learn more than qualifications. That is as true in the last quarter of life as it is in the first three. Laurels are no longer for resting on. A government's first duty is to advise us, truthfully, of what lies ahead, not to make false promises of a risk-free future. Our duty, and yours, is to prepare for that fourth quarter of your life. With proper forethought for the practical details of money and health it can be a time when you are free to be fully yourself, living the kind of life you once dreamed of, full of Ralph Waldo Emerson's recipe for success and the good life that I outlined in my third letter. There will still be time at the end of life to be the person you knew you could be if only circumstances allowed. Well, now they do. That has to be the great boon of our longer lives. I never expected that my later years would be my most enjoyable years, but so it has proved.

There is, however, one essential precondition for a good fourth quarter: your health. You won't enjoy any of those later years if you can't get about and look after yourself. Of course, stuff happens in life that we can't foresee: illness, accidents, unsuspected genetic problems, failing eyesight, dementia perhaps. Old age isn't always nice. But good health in old age starts early. A healthy middle age will make a healthy older age more likely. Obvious, but easy to forget when life is at its busiest. The sad truth is, however, that many will still be too ill, too poor, too unskilled or too depressed to make the best use of these bonus years. This will be a growing challenge for the social services and the NHS. The best contribution that you can make is to do your best to ensure that you will not be in need of their help.

LETTER 20

YOU ARE UNIQUE

THE NEUROLOGIST OLIVER SACKS once said, 'There is no one like anyone else, ever'. You are unique.

Indeed, but who are you? Do you know? How will you know?

I have left these questions to later in my list because they are, in some way, the most searching and the most difficult to answer. The 'white stone' is my answer, but it, as you will discover at the very end of this letter, is only a sort of answer.

One day, several years ago, I was helping my wife put on a show of her photographic works in a small country gallery. It seemed to go well. I was no longer needed. She was showing people around while I was idling in the background.

A man came up to me: 'Lovely photographs, aren't they?' he said. 'Yes, they are,' I agreed.

Then he said, 'Do you know if Charles Handy is here as well as his wife?' 'Yes, he is,' I replied, trying to look modest and unassuming, 'and I am he.' He looked me up and down for a long moment, frowning, clearly puzzled. Then, 'Are you sure?' he said.

It was, I told him, a good question, one that I had been asking myself a lot recently. You see, there had been several versions of Charles Handy as I passed through life. I had started out as an oil executive in South East Asia. Did he know me from those days? In which case he would have found me much altered, and, I hope, much more interesting. Or had he listened to my radio broadcasts on Thought for the Day on Radio 4? I had done these at regular intervals for twenty years. He would not have seen what I looked like but he might have an image in mind from my voice or from the religious nature of that radio slot. So perhaps I now looked far too sleek and secular to be the priestly man he had imagined. Or had he been one of my students forty years before and time had played havoc with the features he remembered?

How or where he remembered me is unimportant. The problem for him, and for me, was that I had changed over time. As we all do. Life changes us; then, hopefully, we change our life to suit us. A further complication is that we can appear to be different people in our different roles. Are you the same person at work that you are at home? How do we know which is the real you?

My wife, the portrait photographer, liked to capture images of her subjects in the three most important roles in their lives. She believed that we each had at least three different selves. She would ask her sitters to act out those selves, dressing the part. She would photograph the three selves separately but in the same space, then put them together so that it looked as if the three selves were talking to each other.

Her own three selves were photographer, family manager, business agent (for me). She was a slightly different person in each. As a photographer she was passionate, focused and brooked no interruption. As the head of the family she was warm, witty and funny, a much-loved granny and a great cook and hostess. Finally as my business manager she was fierce and demanding, wanting nothing but the best for me. She was known as the dragon. So who was she? Obviously a combination of the three but the one that was in the ascendant depended on which stage of life she was in. She would have loved to focus all her time on her photographer self, but family and, later, business matters required her to give time to her other selves.

You too will eventually have three selves of work, passion and home life, three different versions of yourself. They will all be you. The important thing is to recognise that some matter more than others at each stage of life. You can and should experiment in your youth, but as your responsibilities grow you may need to pay more attention to your job or the work you do. It is tempting to think that life can revolve around your enthusiasm or passion, that there can be nothing better than being paid to do what you love. I warn you, however, that if you turn your passion into a business it may become a chore not a pleasure. Had my wife set out to make money from her photography she would have ended up taking wedding photos or endless studies of babies, not what she wanted at all.

I remember meeting a young woman at a party. She wrote plays for television, she told me. I was impressed. 'Don't be,' she said. 'They never get produced.' 'So how do you make a living?' I asked, a bit impertinently. 'I pack eggs on Sundays. No one in their right minds would do it, but it pays well enough and leaves me free in the week.'

It became a byword in our family. If any of us was doing work just for the money we called it 'packing eggs on Sunday' – what you do to keep the bills paid and leave you free to do what you really love. It is very rare to get passion, money and time for home in one package, and even then the money tends to crowd out the others. You can be three selves in one, the personal trinity.

Is there, however, a constant core to the three selves, something that is common to all three that is the true you? We would all like to think that there is, that we don't change our priorities when we change our roles or switch between different selves, but that core self can be hard to pin down.

My wife, creative as always, used her photographic skills to help people work out what was key to their life and what was more incidental. I have mentioned in another letter that she would ask people to choose five objects and a flower to represent their life. She would then ask them to arrange them on a table so that she could photograph them.

The result was what she called a modern still life, like the old Dutch *vanitas* portraits. Those were visual sermons that celebrated a person's wealth but always included a skull or dead leaves or other objects as a reminder that the riches and foibles of the world were all vanities and that death comes to us all in the end. Her portraits were not so morbid in their intention but they did encourage people to work out what was critical to their lives, as they pondered what to put in the centre of their personal picture. You might like to try it.

My own still life had images of my books that were my work, of food and wine and Italy, things that I loved; there was a camera lens to represent my wife and her crucial role in focusing my life, but in the centre was a little yellow gum tree sculpture that looked like two teardrops. The sculpture had been commissioned and given to me by my children, on my seventieth birthday. The teardrops, they told me, were not tears but golden seeds. I had, they said, helped them to find their own golden seeds. The sculpture, therefore, stood for my children and family but also for my deepest belief in the principle of the golden seed that I discussed earlier, the idea that everyone – yes, *everyone* – is special in some way, that there is in all of us a seed of potential. It is my hope for the human race and the heart of my philosophy of life. Put all those symbolic objects together and you have as good a definition of what my life is about as you could get.

That, however, came later in life. It had taken me a long time to discover who I really was. I started at the other end, by crossing out the things that weren't me. I'm ashamed to say that I spent the first ten years of my working life trying to be someone I wasn't – a business manager, for instance. I did not hate the work but I soon knew that I was not going to be any good at it and that I was not particularly interested in it. Nevertheless, no experience in life is ever wasted and when I later started to teach other would-be executives I found that my experience came in useful. As you set off on your life's journey I would urge you to try anything that looks interesting. You will soon find out whether it suits you or not. Even if it proves to be a dead end, or a failure, don't worry. You will learn more from your mistakes than from your successes, as I discovered during my early years at work.

What that meant in practice for me was the need to work out what was important in my life and to distinguish that from what was necessary. The two are different. If you concentrate on what you have to do you may miss out on what you ought to do. I remember, twenty years ago, hearing an Italian journalist being interviewed on BBC radio. The Italian parliament had collapsed, once again, so the BBC interviewer said, 'It is very serious for your country now, is it not?' 'Yes,' replied the Italian, 'it is very serious, but it is not important.' One reason that I love Italy is that they know instinctively what is serious and what is important. It makes governing the country tricky but living in it a delight.

Life is a journey of discovery, I soon found out, a discovery of oneself.

You cannot discover anything, however, if you keep to the old safe and familiar track. You have to explore to discover. Journeys typically have a destination, but explorers have only a hazy notion of what they will discover or where they will end up. Life is like that. I once planted two rows of chestnut trees at the bottom of a field to shield us from traffic noise. A friend, visiting us, commented that it was an avenue of sorts, 'It's an avenue going nowhere,' he added, 'rather like life.' He was, I think, reflecting, half seriously, on his own life, but it could be true of many. Do any of us really know where we are trying to get to in that journey of our life? Or do we only know it when we get there? Perhaps that is what the saying 'death gives meaning to life' is suggesting.

One way of thinking about the destination is to imagine the short eulogy that your best friend might deliver at your funeral, supposing that you lived to a ripe old age. It is a eulogy so no one will speak ill of the dead, and he, or she, is a good friend. The eulogy, therefore, is positive, perhaps with the odd affectionate joke thrown in. What might it say? I have listened to many of these and yes, they do touch on the highlights of long-past achievements, but these were over and done with long ago. Most of the eulogy, therefore, has been about the kind of person he or she was, how they will be remembered, what they leave behind them. It is a slightly bizarre exercise to do when you have only just started out in life, but it does offer another way of thinking about that final destination for the journey.

I keep a white stone on my desk to remind me of a strange verse in the Book of Revelation in the Bible. 'To the one who prevails, the angel said, I will give a white stone on which there will be a name written, a name known only to the one who receives it.'

I don't know what the correct meaning of that verse is but I interpret it to mean that if I succeed in life I will earn a new name that is created especially for me. In other words I will finally be my own person, not just the inheritor of another's name, someone else's genes. It means that if I have made my own mark in some way, lived up to my full potential, made my own life worthwhile, only then do I deserve my white stone. Only you will know if you have earned your white stone. It is personal and private to you. It cannot be defined or marked by honours or public acclaim but you will know it when you get it. I hope you do.

LETTER 21

MY LAST WORDS

LIKE THE POET Keats I have long been 'half in love with easeful death ... to cease upon the midnight with no pain'. But I would also beg a few days when, weak but still coherent, I might have a few hours with my close friends and then, lastly, with you, each of you, my own much-loved grandchildren, one at a time. I would treasure this chance to say goodbye to you.

I feel very privileged to have had the chance to know you. I knew only one of my own grandparents and she died before I was old enough to talk with her. I have been fascinated to watch you grow up and see how you take on the world. You are my legacy, my final gift to the world and I am so proud of you, of all that you have achieved so far in your short lives and of all that you might achieve. I loved the confidence with which you spoke at your grandmother's funeral and celebration. I can see that some of the performance skills of my family have passed down the line. But more importantly I can sense that you already know kindness and thoughtfulness win friends and gain respect. I know that you will do me proud. My only regret is that I will not see you in full flower when you grow up.

It will not be a sad occasion, our meeting. I have had a long and wonderful life, but all things, even good ones, come to an end and I am tired now. Life has been a bit one-legged since your grandmother died and trying to walk alone has been painful. Death I see as one long sleep from which you never wake. I would love to think that in that sleep I might meet your grandmother again in some way but I know it is just wistful dreaming. As it is I talk to her in my head every day and she to me. Death is just the end of a story and, as you know, a story without an end does not work.

When we meet, therefore, I would like to ask you about your hopes for your own story, how you see yourself in ten years' time, doing what and living where, with whom perhaps. I like to think that you and your generation will undo some of the mess that my generation and the one after have left behind. I dare to believe that your values will be better than ours were, that you will be less selfish, less heedless of those less fortunate than you, more aware of the environment and the need to protect it, that you will be kinder than we were and more tolerant of those who live differently.

In our defence we lived in a different time. We came of age soon after the last war ended. We felt sure that, like the previous generations, we would be at war again within twenty years, only with new enemies and with new and worse weapons. Two of my classmates had already died in the Korean War of the 1950s and every man had done two years in the armed services as their National Service. The spirit of war was all around us. I felt it was almost inevitable that I would be dead by the time I was thirty. No wonder, looking back, that we were selfish and short-sighted, eager to pluck what we could out of life before it ended. After twenty years, in the late sixties, life began again, hope blossomed and nations competed to get to the moon not to war. But by then I was a married man with two children and a wife to support.

By comparison, you are fortunate. You can reasonably expect to live into your late nineties. You are unlikely to have to fight in any wars, unless you choose to. You can expect to be healthy if you take care of yourself. You will be more broadly educated that I was and will have a more enriching home life. That is not to criticise my own parents, who had to bring me up in wartime, in an impoverished country with few facilities and no access to the modern marvels of the internet and television. You will be able to go where you want, do what you choose, live with whom you like, even decide what gender you want to be seen as. It is a world with much more freedom than I knew even if there are still some traces of prejudice to be seen.

Of course, the other side of freedom is insecurity. I will long remember my first visit to Moscow in 1961. Few people went there then. The only flight available was on Aeroflot from Copenhagen. As a private tourist I had to be escorted everywhere by an Intourist guide. Luckily she was an attractive young woman of my age. We got on well. At one stage she asked me, 'Is it true that in your country you have to find your own work and your own place to live?' 'Yes,' I replied, 'we call it freedom.' 'I think that's terrifying,' she said.

She was right. To move from an organised society to one of individual freedom must be frightening.

In my day, Britain was semi-organised. There were traditional industries and large organisations that offered work and training to most of the population. You had to apply but jobs were not scarce.

Sons followed fathers down the mines or to the steelworks. Businesses offered lifetime careers. The armed services were eager employers as were the government services. I was spoilt for choice as were all of my age group, no matter what their level of education.

It was freedom with the promise of security.

That promise no longer exists. There is always work to be done and work to be found but more of it has to be organised by yourself. That is the new cost of freedom. I hope that some of the ideas in these letters may help. Trust yourself, don't be afraid to make mistakes, be honest even if it costs you, remember the proverb that happiness (in Aristotle's sense of happiness) is having something to work on, something to hope for and someone to love.

And now for some practical tips – or, more accurately, the things I wish that I had done, so please do them for me.

Learn a foreign language fluently. You can only do this by going to live and work in the country concerned. It does not matter which language, although Mandarin and Spanish would be the most useful. It helps, I am told, if you fall in love with a local, as long as he or she does not use you as their English teacher. I never learnt any language well enough to have prolonged conversation. I left it too late and I have always regretted it. Yes, everyone speaks English but you cannot know someone unless you can speak with them in their own tongue.

Learn to play a musical instrument while you are young. Music and mathematics are the two international languages. Anyone anywhere can read them without translation, and they are connected. I remember only too well my shame when my six-year-old son asked me for help with reading his piano score and I confessed that I could not. 'What?' he said, amazed. 'Can't you read, Daddy?' To him, everyone could read music as well as letters. It has allowed him access to another world, one that I can appreciate but not understand.

Learn an individual sport while you are young. Team sports are great but they begin to peter out when you leave school or college unless you are a professional or talented amateur. The individual sports, however – tennis, golf, badminton, even croquet – last throughout life and can be a special way to combine activity and friendship. I learnt my tennis too late, got into bad habits and was never any good. I regret that now.

Write a diary. Marcus Aurelius, one of the great Roman emperors, who lived in the second century AD, kept a diary in which he recorded not his daily doings but what he learnt from them and how he prepared for the challenges ahead. He called it his *Meditations*. I strongly recommend that you read them sometime. More importantly, copy him. I long ago discovered that I had to write to find out what I thought. A weekly look back at what you have been doing and could have done better, or your thoughts on the point of it all, will greatly improve your ability to set the right priorities for your work and life. What worked for the emperor might work for you.

Fall in love. To find that you care for another more than for oneself is a marvellous experience. When you give of yourself for another you will find a deeper fulfilment than any more ordinary pleasure. You may do it several times. I did. You don't have to marry the first or the second or even any at all, although, as I have written, I have found the bonds of marriage to be very strengthening. I am not talking sex here.

Lust is not love, however appealing it may be at times. Please do not confuse the two, and never marry for lust.

Remember Aristotle's virtues, particularly that of courage, to stand up for what you believe, no matter what. But remember, too, his golden mean, that too much courage can turn into arrogance.

These days employers look for character more than technical skills, believing that they can teach the latter but that character is there to begin with. Aristotle's list is the best definition of character that I know.

And so farewell, to you and all those others who may read these letters.

May your lives be fulfilling, worthwhile and enjoyable, and at the end may you have no regrets for what you left undone.

ACKNOWLEDGEMENTS

It is one thing to write a book, but quite another to publish it. The subtle hints from my agent, Toby Mundy, first brought the idea to life, while the creative eye, careful management and painstaking attention to detail of Nigel Wilcockson, my editor at Penguin Random House, made it a book. I am hugely grateful to both of them and to all those who worked behind the scenes at my publishers to help them.

My wife, Elizabeth, died before it was finished but she had hugely encouraged me to write it. Her ideas and values permeate these letters. Her influence on my life and my thinking has been profound, something for which my gratitude is deep and enduring.

Charles Handy is an independent writer, broadcaster and teacher. He has been an oil executive, an economist, a professor at the London Business School, the Warden of St. George's House in Windsor Castle and the chairman of the Royal Society for the Encouragement of Arts, Manufacture and Commerce. He was born in Co. Kildare in Ireland, the son of an archdeacon, and educated in Ireland, England (Oxford University) and the USA (Massachusetts Institute of Technology). His many books include *The Empty Raincoat*, *Understanding Organizations*, *Gods of Management*, *The Future of Work*, *Waiting for the Mountain to Move* and *The Second Curve*. He lives in London and Norfolk.